S0-BCN-944

THE GREAT TEA ROOMS
of AMERICA

THE GREAT TEA ROOMS
of AMERICA

Text and Photographs by
Bruce Richardson

BENJAMIN PRESS

Other tea books by Bruce & Shelley Richardson:
A Year of Teas at the Elmwood Inn
A Tea for All Seasons
The Tea Table
The New Tea Companion
The Great Tea Rooms of Britain
Looking Deeply Into Tea
Tea in the City: New York
Tea in the City: London
Tea in the City: Paris

Fourth Edition © 2008 by Bruce Richardson
Third Edition © 2006 by Bruce Richardson
Second Edition © 2003 by Bruce Richardson
Original Copyright © 2002 by Bruce Richardson
Photographs Copyright © by Bruce Richardson

Additional photographs courtesy of Butchart Gardens (pages 18, 19, 20, 21),
Grand American Hotel (pages 50, 53),
pages 26-29 used by permission of Disney Enterprises, Inc.

Senior Editor: Freear Williams
Photo Editor: Ben Richardson

BENJAMIN PRESS
P. O. Box 100
Perryville, Kentucky 40468 USA
800.765.2139
www.benjaminpress.com

ISBN 978-0-9793431-5-5

Printed in China through
Four Colour Imports

All Rights Reserved. No part of this work, in whole or in part,
may be reproduced by any means without prior written
permission of the copyright holder.

Acknowledgements

Choosing the tea rooms to go into this collection has been a daunting task for each of the four editions. Fellow tea blender John Harney suggested I do this book shortly after I published the first edition of *The Great Tea Rooms of Britain* in 1997. At the time, I told him that I doubted there were enough tea rooms in America to justify a book. That changed dramatically over the past decade as hundreds of tea rooms sprang up coast to coast. That vital resurgence of interest in tea rooms brought a number of distinguished venues to the forefront of America's tea culture.

The second challenge in producing this book was the task of travelling great distances to visit tea rooms. Researching my British book was easily accomplished by driving across England, Scotland, and Wales. Often my photographer and I would cruise the countryside hoping to stumble upon a remarkable tea room in some remote village. This was not possible in America. Preparing the first edition included 12 tours, nearly 100,000 air miles, numerous trains, and countless rental cars in a three year span. I once visited six Southern California tea rooms in 48 hours and had tea and scones in each! With this fourth edition, four new tea rooms have been added and four have been removed, mainly due to closings.

I met hospitable hosts at every stop. They took time from their busy schedules to prepare food shots. They sat down over a cup of tea to talk about how hard they worked. They even cleaned up the occasional broken teacup knocked over by my gangly tripods. Tea room owners are the most accommodating and gracious people you will ever meet. I'm sure that's why they are in the tea business.

Throughout this project I have received suggestions from people who wanted their favorite tea room included. Some tea rooms owners and friends called asking if they were going to be in the book. Unfortunately, I couldn't investigate and photograph every location brought to my attention. This is by no means a "top tea room" list. My aim is to give readers an overview of different tea room styles represented across the country. My selections have been confirmed by countless conversations I have had with professionals in the tea trade and, in large part, through comments from the readers of my books.

There will be opportunities for additional inclusions in future editions so please contact me with any suggestions.

My thanks go to my editor, Freear Williams. My son, Ben served as my photographer's assistant, traveling partner, and photo editor. My sincerest gratitude goes to my loyal readers who use my books as they travel the world with tea on their minds.

Bruce Richardson

Mac Nab's Tea Room, Boothbay, Maine

THE GREAT TEA ROOMS
of AMERICA

Introduction

Americans have a great affection for tea. The ancient beverage and all its trappings may not be as ingrained in our social habits as in Great Britain or China, but it has played a defining role in shaping the culture and politics of our young nation.

America's love affair with tea was born from her British and Dutch heritages. William Penn introduced tea drinking to the Quaker colony that he founded in Delaware in 1682. Within a few years, the arriving immigrants brought with them tea rituals that had been a part of the cultures in their homelands. By 1757, tea had become such a vital part of society that Manhattan established special "tea water pumps" and the City of New York enacted a law for "the tea water men."

The love of tea was so great that, in the years leading up to the Revolution, the per capita consumption of tea in America was greater than in England. The problem was that all tea brought into the colonies passed through English hands and was heavily taxed by King George II. "The women of the colonies will pay any price for their beloved tea," he is rumored to have said. King George's tax scheme failed and the women revolted. Patriotic fervor spread down the eastern seaboard and indignant women signed pledges to never again drink the King's tea. They didn't go as far as to forgo the ritual of tea time, they simply replaced the tea leaves with local herbs and infusions such as sassafras or raspberry vine.

The young ladies of Boston signed a pledge stating, "We the daughters of those patriots who have, and do now appear for the public interest, and in that principally regard their posterity, as such do with pleasure engage with them in denying ourselves the drinking of foreign tea, in hopes to frustrate a plan that tends to deprive a whole community of all that is valuable to life."

The following verses enjoyed a wide circulation:

A Lady's Adieu to Her Tea-Table

FAREWELL the Tea-board with your gaudy attire,
Ye cups and ye saucers that I did admire;
To my cream pot and tongs I now bid adieu
That pleasure's all fled that I once found in you.
Farewell pretty chest that so lately did shine,
With hyson and congo and best double fine;
Many a sweet moment by you I have sat,
Hearing girls and old maids to tattle and chat;
And the spruce coxcomb laugh at nothing at all,
Only some silly work that might happen to fall.
No more shall my teapot so generous be
In filling the cups with this pernicious tea,
For I'll fill it with water and drink out the same,
Before I'll lose LIBERTY that dearest name,
Because I am taught (and believe it is fact)
That our ruin is aimed at in the late act,
Of imposing a duty on all foreign Teas,
Which detestable stuff we can quit when we please.
LIBERTY'S The Goddess that I do adore,
And I'll maintain her right until my last hour,
Before she shall part I will die in the cause,
For I'll never be govern'd by tyranny's laws.

Independence fever swelled to the boiling point on the evening of December 16, 1773 when three English cargo ships were boarded by irate citizens in Boston Harbor. Dressed as Mohawk Indians, they took only three hours to empty the contents of 342 tea chests that contained Chinese leaf teas, including Bohea, Souchong, Hyson, and Congou, into the seawater. In retaliation, Parliament passed "The Five Intolerable Acts," one of which closed Boston Harbor until the ruined tea was paid for. The Boston Tea Party was one of several "tea dumpings" that took place in major ports along the eastern seaboard.

Following the Revolutionary War, America staked its own claim in the tea trade, thanks in large part to the development of fast-sailing tea ships modeled after the Baltimore clippers. These American marvels made the arduous trip to China and back in only 180 days. By the turn of the twentieth century, tea had become a source of social congregation. In both America and England, fine hotels housed tea courts and tea rooms where men and women could gather in the late afternoon, sip tea, and exchange pleasantries. These tea rooms and tea courts soon moved to host tea dances, where spirits soared over the freedom and conveniences afforded by the ever evolving technology of the day.

When you ask someone to describe an American tea room today you will likely get a variety of answers. A tea room in Alabama means something different than a tea room in British Columbia. A hotel tea in New York might have little resemblance to an Asian tea room in Washington, D.C. Much of what America knows about tea rooms came about

in the 1920s and 30s when we became a nation on wheels. As people became mobile, small restaurants and cafes sprang up along the highways to feed the growing number of tourists. Many of these privately owned eateries were owned and operated by women who had well-honed skills in cooking and hospitality. They had spent much of their lives cooking for large families and countless church suppers. They would sometimes renovate rundown buildings or cottages and give them a charming low-budget decorating scheme using readily-available furnishings and fabrics. The dining rooms were decorated in a feminine style to appeal to the women who were traveling in great numbers. One drawback was that these frilly female sanctuaries were not always alluring to businessmen. Duncan Hines once said that "men's phobia about tea rooms makes them miss a lot of good eating."

The simple menus included home cooked items such as chicken salad or baked ham that were perfect for a light luncheon. The highlight of the meal was the homemade breads or rich desserts. The drink of choice was usually tea - cold, not hot. This type of establishment is still common across the southern United States. A recent directory of tea rooms in Texas lists 160 such establishments. It would be difficult to find a hot cup of loose tea and an English scone in many of them but, without a doubt, most will offer a version of chicken salad and iced tea.

Two serendipitous happenings led to the proliferation of iced tea. The first icebox patent was issued in 1830 and cold tea recipes began appearing in community cookbooks such as *The Kentucky Housewife* and *Housekeeping in Old Virginia*.

One of the most reported ice tea stories came from the 1904 St. Louis World's Fair when Richard Blechynden, a tea vendor, became weary of selling his cups of hot tea in the summer heat. He dropped ice in the beverage in an attempt to boost sales. His gimmick worked and refreshed fairgoers took the simple recipe home.

A second invention occurred in 1908 when Thomas Sullivan began to ship tea samples in individual bags to New York restaurants. He found that restaurants were preparing the tea samples without

Chelseas, Asheville, North Carolina

extracting the tea from the bag. Hence, bagged tea was born, allowing a tea drinkers to effortlessly produce a hot cup of tea on demand.

One of America's top ten tea rooms during the 1930s was the McDonald's Tea Room in Gallatin, Missouri (no relation to the golden arches found today). Virginia McDonald's fame and baking prowess was spread by news media across the country, including *The Saturday Evening Post*. Her advice for young brides? "I think any girl who really is interested in making a success of her marriage should learn to be a good cook," she said.

An interesting offshoot of this boom in tea rooms was the appearance of cooking schools devoted to tea room management. One of the largest was the Tea Room Institute of Washington, D.C., founded in 1916. These culinary entrepreneurs offered a convenient home study program entitled "Pouring Tea for Profit" that promised graduates the opportunity to make the incredible sum of $35 to $50 per week as a tea room manager. The position was described as "a pleasant, dignified, enjoyable profession that gives you an enviable social position in the community and commands the respect and admiration of all who know you."

Following a post War World II decline in the consumption of tea, America rediscovered the ancient beverage in the 1990s. The number of tea rooms and sales of gourmet teas began to grow steadily as more and more tea companies entered the market. Tea room seminars, tea books and tea conferences now are popular topics at any gourmet food show. Over 150 tea companies may be found in the United States and Canada.

Many Americans had their first taste of well-made tea overseas. They enjoyed tea at hotels such as The Ritz in London or The Peninsula in Hong Kong. Upon returning home, they sought out tea rooms and tea shops that allowed them to recreate that satisfying and refined tea time tradition.

Leading this second American Tea Revolution are a number of outstanding tea venues in Canada and the United States where the art of tea is taken to greater heights. The emphasis here is on the celebration of afternoon tea, that elegant multi-coursed mid-afternoon affair first brought to life by the British. Not to be confused with high tea (a common English supper taken with a pot of tea at a high dining table), this event is aimed first at satisfying the spirit, then the appetite.

One refreshing aspect of American tea rooms is the eclectic mix of cuisines from which tea room chefs choose. No longer confined to the traditional egg salad or cucumber sandwiches, American tea rooms offer a wide variety of savory and sweet selections drawing on traditions from all parts of the world. The recipes found in this collection are indicative of the vast array of delicious foods available to modern tea room patrons.

Guests now choose from tea lists that resemble wine lists at fine restaurants. The standard offerings of English Breakfast and Earl Grey have been joined by First and Second Flush Darjeelings, green teas, white teas, oolongs and infusions. Tea customers are becoming sophisticated in their choosing thanks to articles about tea that regularly appear in magazines and newspapers.

As is the case in Britain, American tea rooms are found in a myriad locations. Besides the grand hotels in major cities, tea is being served in cozy inns, bed & breakfasts, restored mansions, farm houses and cottages. The tea locations found in this book cater not just to women, but also to men. Tea room owners are realizing that to be successful, they need to create an inviting environment where men feel equally comfortable.

Most of all, the popularity of afternoon tea can be linked to the fact that Americans are looking for a respite from fast food, cell phones and abrupt service. At an outstanding tea room, the pace should be relaxed, the surroundings serene, and the service attentive. The customer should leave with his or her soul refreshed - much like exiting a religious ceremony. A great tea room is not just a restaurant, it is a sanctuary from our fast-paced society.

Fairmont Chateau Banff Springs, Banff, Alberta

The Fairmont Hotel, San Francisco, California

THE GREAT TEA ROOMS OF AMERICA

TABLE OF CONTENTS

ALICE'S TEA CUP

New York, New York

Alice may have fallen down a rabbit hole to reach her mad tea party, but you'll only have to step down a short flight of stairs to enter one of New York's most colorful tea rooms. Sisters Haley and Lauren Fox, life-long tea lovers, have created a wonderland in the upper West Side where everyone seems to feel welcome.

Their concept was born in 2001, when the women, native New York City West Siders, were living in Los Angeles. Haley worked in film production, while Lauren was, and still is, an actress. They visited a tea house, and wondered how such a place might fare back home.

For some New Yorkers, lattes and cappuccinos just don't cut it. They prefer whistling kettles, irresistible aromas and the serenity of a perfectly steeped cup of tea. They have found their hideaway at Alice's Tea Cup. On any given day, an eclectic group of tea lovers fills the two cozy dining rooms. Mothers with small children, aspiring actors, tourists, and neighborhood regulars gather for conversation and camaraderie over a cup of tea. The Raspberry Room often becomes a private alcove for bachelorette parties, wedding showers, or their famous "un-birthday parties."

The misconception that New Yorkers are hardened and serious falls by the wayside in this land of make-believe. Perhaps guests feel comfortable because the décor is cheerfully casual. Cream-colored walls are decorated with whimsical quotes: W*e're all mad here!* and *Tea time is quiet time. Off with your cell phone or off with your head!*

The actors in this outrageous scenario are seated at mismatched wooden tables and chairs or lounging on floral-patterned banquettes. Aspiring "Alices" may choose from a selection of colorful party dresses that await them as they make their way through the narrow hallway.

Although the atmosphere may seem playful and carefree, the owners are serious about their tea. Guests may choose from 120 types of loose tea. All teas are brewed in double-filtered water and served in a china pot, equipped with a decorative sponge drip-catcher.

Several set teas are offered. The combinations all have whimsical names such as *The Nibble, The Mad Hatter, The Jabberwocky,* or *The Wee Tea.* Alice's scones are huge and almost a meal on their own. The flavors change daily with pumpkin being one of the most popular.

The eccentric menu delights your mind even before your physical hunger is satisfied. The menu reads like a fairy book with "Sweets and treats for the Alice in all of us." These include such delights as chai crème brulee, mocha chocolate-chip cake, Verveine tea-infused lemon tart, raspberry-mint tea sorbet, Tahitian vanilla gelato, chocolate mousse, s'mores, mixed berries with homemade Chantilly crème and lavender honey, or a vanilla ice cream sandwich served on a peanut butter chocolate chip cookie. There is even a daily puree just for babies.

New Yorkers can't get enough of the enchantment this wonderland brings to the maddening pace of the city. In 2005, the sisters opened Alice's Chapter Two tea house at 156 E. 64th Street and Lexington Avenue and, in 2007, they launched Chapter Three at 220 E. 81st Street. All are equally as whimsical as the original edition across Central Park.

Haley and Lauren spent years traveling to tea rooms around the world, dreaming of the time they would open their own tea house in New York City. Their dream has come true and they have made "Alices" of us all.

Touring suggestions: The original Alice's Tea Cup sits just off Columbus Avenue within easy walking distance of the American Museum of Natural History. What better family outing could there be than to spend a couple of hours at the museum and then unwind over tea and scones at Alice's?

Don't miss the Hayden Planetarium located on the north side of the museum. It is unlike any other such facility in the world. In the top half of the Hayden Sphere, the most technologically advanced space theater in existence uses advanced visual technology to create shows of unparalleled sophistication, realism, and excitement. With this high-definition system, the Hayden Planetarium is the largest and most powerful virtual reality simulator in the world.

Housed in glass and steel, the sphere, with its clear enclosure, is as awe inspiring from the exterior as it is from the interior, especially when lit from the inside at night. The museum faces Central Park.

The two newer Alice's Tea Cup locations are across Central Park near Lexington Avenue. Chapter Three is easily accessible by exiting the subway at Hunter College. From here you can walk south and shop at Bloomingdales before tea time or head northwest to the Frick Museum to enjoy one of the best and most intimate art collections in Manhattan.

The Frick Collection includes some of the best-known paintings by the greatest European artists, major works of sculpture (among them one of the finest groups of small bronzes in the world), superb 18th century French furniture and porcelains, Limoges enamels, Oriental rugs, and other works of remarkable quality. The collection is housed in the original Frick mansion. It is easy to navigate and an hour here will leave your mind refreshed, your soul inspired and your body in need of a good cup of tea and something sweet to finish a perfectly sophisticated afternoon.

Alice's Chapter Two lies farther north and closer to the Metropolitan Museum of Art.

The Met is one of the great museums of the world that can only be enjoyed in small bites at a time. Plan on spending a couple of hours to see the highlights that you mapped out in advance. Afterwards, the front steps are a great place to people watch. On a sunny day, you might think most of New York is soaking in the sunshine here. Artists set up shop on the sidewalk along the Central Park wall where they display their creations for sale to starry-eyed tourists.

Pass up the Fifth Avenue hot dog vendors and cap your day's adventure with tea at Alice's. Or, if French tea is more your liking, walk down Lexington Avenue to Payard at 74th Street. Make your way through the display cases filled with unbelievably exquisite pastries and chocolates and take a table in the dining room where you may enjoy your afternoon tea steeped in an Asian iron pot. How sophisticated! Don't forget to indulge your sweet tooth by tasting a few truffles or a pear tart. You'll think you are in a salon du thé along Paris' Left Bank.

BUTCHART GARDENS

Victoria, British Columbia

In 1904, Robert Butchart began manufacturing Portland Cement at Tod Inlet on Vancouver Island, 21 miles north of Victoria. In 1904, he and his family established their home there. As he exhausted the limestone in the quarry near their house, his enterprising wife, Jenny, conceived an unprecedented plan for refurbishing the bleak pit that resulted. She requisitioned tons of topsoil from farmland nearby, had it brought to Tod Inlet by horse and cart, and used it to line the floor of the abandoned quarry. With the help of her husband's workers, and under her personal supervision, the abandoned quarry bloomed as the spectacular Sunken Garden.

The plant stopped manufacturing cement in 1916, but continued to make tiles and flower pots as late as 1950. A single kiln chimney now overlooks the quarry Mrs. Butchart so miraculously reclaimed.

Mr. Butchart took great pride in his wife's remarkable work. He collected ornamental birds amongst her ravishing flowers; trained pigeons at the site of the present Begonia Bower; ducks in the Star Pond; noisy peacocks on the front lawn; and a curmudgeon of a parrot in the main house. By 1908, reflecting their own world travels, the Butcharts had created a Japanese Garden on the

seaside of their home, and later constructed a symmetrical Italian Garden on the site of their former tennis court. The fine Rose Garden replaced a large kitchen vegetable patch in 1929.

The renown of Mrs. Butchart's gardening quickly spread. By the 1920s, more than 50,000 people came each year to see her creation. She was a generous hostess, not only to her own friends but to hundreds of visitors to Victoria. In appreciation of her generosity, in 1931 she was named Victoria's best citizen. Between them, Jennie and Robert Butchart seemed to come up with a magical formula that brought many people great happiness. In a gesture toward all their visitors, the hospitable Butcharts christened their estate "Benvenuto," the Italian word for "Welcome."

Their house grew into a comfortable, luxurious showplace, with a bowling alley, indoor saltwater swimming pool, paneled billiard room and - wonder of its age! - a self-playing Aeolian pipe organ. Today the residence contains the Dining Room Restaurant, some offices, and rooms still used for private entertaining.

Butchart Gardens has grown to be the premier West Coast display garden, while maintaining the gracious traditions of the past. Nearly one million

people visit each year, enjoying the floral beauty, entertainment and lighting programs.

Butchart Gardens today has established an international reputation for continuously flowering plants. Each year over one million bedding plants in over 700 varieties are used throughout the Gardens to ensure uninterrupted bloom from March through October.

The custom of serving tea was started by Jennie Butchart in the early 1900s, making the Gardens host to Victoria's oldest and best-loved tea tradition. In the spirit of the founders' hospitality, both afternoon and high teas are served year-round in the original Butchart home and seasonally in the stunning Italian Garden.

Afternoon tea begins with a colorful seasonal berry trifle topped with chantilly cream. The meal combines a little of the High Tea tradition with a warm sausage roll and shrimp with Gruyère quiche. A tiered tray of freshly-made tea sandwiches then follows. The sandwiches offered are some of the most innovative tea time creations to be found and

include locally smoked wild salmon with maple and whole grain mustard cream cheese, smoked honey ham on a rosemary and cheddar biscuit, mango curry chicken roulade, and cucumber with ginger cream cheese.

Homemade sweets include Grand Marnier truffles, chocolate barquette with fresh fruit, raspberry marzipan Napoleons, and lemon and poppy seed loaf. Fresh candied ginger scones with berry jam and whipped Devon cream round out the menu.

A large pot of loose leaf tea complements your meal. Among the varieties offered you'll find Gardens Blend (light black tea blend of Darjeeling, Black Yunnan and Gunpowder), Bachelor Button (Chinese black and Sencha tea flavored with bergamot, rhubarb and blue cornflowers), Teaberry Blend (Ceylon tea flavored with strawberries, raspberries, blackberries and currants) and Rose Congou. These blends are also available in the gift shop.

For hearty eaters, Butchart Gardens offers The High Tea, complete with the addition of Cornish pasties, salmon rolls, savory herb potato scones and toasted crumpets.

The enjoyment of all these beautiful and delicious foods is enhanced by the stunning vistas seen through the Butchart home's windows. The deep-blue Canadian sky serves as a tranquil backdrop to the innumerable shades of green found in the classic Italian gardens below.

"An old garden is like an old friend. As with old friends memories come and certain spots give memories forever dear." This adage is carried out with sweet detail in the gardens surrounding the former Butchart home.

On an island whose climate and rich soil nurture spectacular floral beauty, guests find the scenery sweetened even more with the addition of an outstanding afternoon tea. It is one of the great memories of a visit to Victoria - both for the eye and the soul.

CLIFFSIDE INN

Newport, Rhode Island

Newport has long been the retreat of America's rich and famous. The Vanderbilt and Astor families knew a good place to put down roots. After all, they developed Palm Beach, the Hudson Valley and the Berkshires for seasonal getaways.

By the 1860s, it was not fashionable for wealthy families to stay at a Newport hotel for the summer season. One must own or rent a cottage. Most of the bigger hotels closed while more cottages were being built. Due to the travel limitations of the Civil War, cottagers hailing from New York and Boston dominated summer society. Newport attracted not only America's financial elite, but many of its most gifted artists, writers, educators, scientists, politicians and architects. The day was spent playing croquet, tennis, sailing, or listening to band concerts on the lawn.

These summer homes, or cottages, were generally shingle-clad resort architecture inspired by the contemporary British Queen Anne style and American Colonial buildings. By the late 1900s, an entirely different taste took over. Grand new cottages were built in a palatial scale. This rush to opulence, led by families such as the Vanderbilts, made Newport the place in America to experience the Gilded Age. William Vanderbilt set the standard for future building in 1892 when he opened Marble House as a gift for

his wife, Alva. On fashionable Bellevue Avenue, it was the finest summer house money could buy.

It cost William Vanderbilt $11 million to build and decorate Marble House, but Alva divorced him four years after the project was finished. She got the house, which she closed soon after marrying William's friend and neighbor. When her second husband died, Alva discovered the cause of female suffrage, and reopened Marble House in 1909 to hold benefit teas. Teapots in the scullery bear the phrase "Votes for Women." She went so far as to build her own Chinese Teahouse in 1913, overlooking the Cliff Walk next to the sea.

Further down Cliff Walk stands one of Newport's premier inns and a setting for one of New England's finest afternoon teas, The Cliffside Inn.

In a city known for eccentricity, Cliffside Inn was once the home of Newport's most peculiar and mysterious personality, Beatrice Turner. The wealthy and hauntingly beautiful artist had a reputation as being an eccentric recluse. In the early 1900s, as styles changed, she and her mother continued to dress in Victorian clothes. Following her father's death in 1913, she had her fabulous Newport home painted black. It remained that color for 45 years.

After Beatrice died in 1948, executors of the estate opened the neglected and decaying home to

former television journalist soon discovered that the house had once been filled with the images of Beatrice.

Baker has accumulated many paintings by Beatrice through the years. Once again, they fill the halls and adorn every guest room. Many of the larger canvases hang in the parlor where they look down at guests enjoying afternoon tea. His fascination with the Turner story led him to commission and publish a book on the artist's life entitled *Beatrice: The Untold Story of a Legendary Woman of Mystery.*

The ritual of afternoon tea is featured in the diary entries carefully kept by Beatrice. She speaks often of taking tea in both her family home in Philadelphia and her beloved Cliffside.

Baker and his talented staff have turned Cliffside Inn into one of the most celebrated lodgings in Newport. Thirteen guest suites are found in the main house, each completely refurbished with working fireplaces and furnished with elegant antiques.

find every room of the three-story mansion piled high with paintings. The vast majority were self-portraits. She painted herself sitting, standing, at home, on the town, in evening gowns, in dressing gowns, and after her mother died, she painted herself in the nude.

Unable to sell the paintings, most were burned in a bonfire at the Newport dump. Fortunately, a roguish New York attorney rescued 70 artworks from the fire and took them on tour. The tour was unsuccessful but journalists found the story fascinating. The Hearst newspapers printed the legend of Beatrice Turner in 1949 and Life magazine followed with a photo spread in 1950. The paintings then disappeared.

When Winthrop P. Baker acquired Cliffside Inn, he was impressed by the detailed architecture of the house with its Victorian turrets, gabled roof and grand porch. He also was smitten by the 1921 double portrait of Beatrice Turner and her mother hanging in the parlor. His curiosity aroused, the

An adjacent cottage contains two more impressive rooms. "Our goal," he relates, "is to make the Cliffside Inn equally, if not better, known for its afternoon teas." Inspired by Beatrice's love of afternoon tea, the staff has researched and recreated a daily tea event worthy of the Newport tradition.

Each afternoon, a complete array of tea foods are set for the inn's guests. (You must be an overnight guest in order to partake.) The beautiful display of tea foods include such delicacies as strawberry almond tartlets, shortbread, scones with curds and cream, cucumber sandwiches, crab-stuffed mushrooms, angels on horseback, chocolate dipped fruits, assorted French pastries and a selection of hot teas and iced teas.

Guests may linger as long as they like and enjoy the refreshments to their hearts', and appetites', content. Resting on the Victorian sofas beside the bay window or in the high backed chairs in front of the fireplace makes the event a luxurious respite following a long day traipsing through mansions or shopping in the old town area.

Surely the Vanderbilts, the Astors, and even Beatrice Turner spent many leisurely afternoons enjoying fine "Newport Teas." It is doubtful that any could have been more satisfying or more elegant than the afternoon tea presented today at the Cliffside Inn.

Touring suggestions: A drive down Bellevue Avenue is one of the first things you must do when visiting Newport for the first time. The sight of all this opulence can be overwhelming. The Breakers, Marble House, and The Elms are three great houses to visit first. The Newport Preservation Society handles all the ticketing. Several tour packages are available through the Society's website.

Be sure to take a stroll in the late afternoon along Cliff Walk. This seaside walkway gives you a free glimpse into the backyards of many of these fine "cottages."

The heart of old Newport is filled with historical walks, restaurants, shops, and boutiques that make this a premier vacation destination.

DISNEY'S GRAND FLORIDIAN RESORT & SPA

Walt Disney World Resort
Lake Buena Vista, Florida

It is no surprise that the people who specialize in making magical kingdoms also know how to create beautiful afternoon tea. Guests at Walt Disney World's Grand Floridian Resort realize the Garden View Tea Lounge is the perfect spot for relaxing during a busy Disney vacation. This civilized haven offers solitude and refined service for weary adults who have explored Epcot, the Magic Kingdom and MGM Studios to the point of fatigue. There are no lines here, no children tugging at your sleeve, no weather worries. The biggest decision you make all afternoon is what kind of tea you will have.

Disney's Grand Floridian Resort and Spa has the feel of a grand Victorian hotel on a tropical island. The resort opened in August 1988 and is considered the flagship of all Disney resorts. The 933-room facility located on the shores of Seven Seas Lagoon is southwest, and one monorail stop, from the Magic Kingdom. The great white wooden main building features a spectacular red gabled roof and a five-story Grand Lobby.

Guest stepping into the Grand Lobby are swept back into Queen Victoria's day: spacious verandahs, crystal chandeliers, stained-glass ceiling, exotic aviary, and nine-foot ebony grand piano. A grand staircase leads to the second floor where comfortable sitting areas await guests with tired feet. Uniformed bellmen and courteous guest relations personnel are plentiful, looking after every possible need.

The Tea Lounge sits at the end of the Grand Lobby. The coral walls, white woodwork, and splendid gold mirrors lend a gentle calm to the island motif. An entire wall of tall arched windows let in the bright Florida sunshine and give an unobstructed view of the floral gardens, pools, and beaches that fill the grounds. It's not uncommon to see brides in wedding dresses trailed by ladies in waiting and countless photographers walking through the outdoor gardens. The popular Fairy Tale Wedding Pavilion sits on a private island in the lagoon.

The lounge is filled with a variety of marble-topped tables and comfortable upholstered arm chairs. Each table is set with Royal Albert China. An impressive floral display crowns a draped round double-tiered table filled with trays of delicious pastries, bowls of strawberries and cream, and colorful English trifle. White wooden trolleys are topped with rows of teapots waiting to be filled with piping hot water and fine loose teas. Two signature teas for the hotel are Gardenview Blend with sweet jasmine and citrus bergamot and the Princess Breakfast Tea with vanilla bean, South African organic rooibos, and a hint of strawberries. Other interesting choices include Osmanthus Oolong, Eros, Cassis, or Mad Hatter.

A variety of tea meals for all appetites are offered in the Tea Lounge. The Grand Tea is a classic traditional English afternoon menu offering a variety of tea sandwiches, scones, tarts, pastries, English trifle, tea and champagne. The sandwich selections are always changing but they often include egg & chive, salmon spread, watercress and cucumber, and chicken with almonds.

The Buckingham Palace service includes sandwiches, scones, jam tarts, strawberries with cream and tea. The lighter Sally Lunn Tea is similar to a quick English Cream Tea featuring Sally Lunn rolls with apricot preserves, strawberries and cream, and a pot of tea.

One unique menu choice is the Prince Edward's Gentlemen's Tea. This savory offering seems intent on coaxing novice male tea drinkers into a venue often dominated by women. The Disney chefs have put together a fantastic presentation of duck liver en croute, country pâté, potted crab crostini and marinated fresh berries, all served with a delicious Cumberland sauce. Scones with Devonshire cream accompany the feast, along with a pot of tea and a glass of port. Close your eyes while eating and you can imagine yourself in a fine country house hotel in England's Lake District.

Even children can experience some of the charms that the Grand Floridian has to offer in one of its most recent offerings, the Wonderland Tea Party. At this pint-size tea party, guests from 3 to 10 years of age will hear stories, have a little lunch and be entertained by some Disney characters known to participate in a famous tea party of their own. The children will take a "hands-on" approach to their dining as they finger-paint and decorate their own cupcakes and munch on heart-shaped peanut butter and jam sandwiches. Chocolate dipped Rice Krispie squares, and the Grand Floridian's special brand of children's tea is also served.

Also for the younger "tea lover" in your party is a meal named "Mrs. Potts Tea," that includes a variety of tea sandwiches such as tuna salad, ham and cheese and peanut butter and jelly on white bread.

The Grand Floridian atmosphere is elegant, but in a friendly Disney way. Guests are made to feel special and appreciated. They often leave refreshed and inspired. The Grand Floridian transports you to a magical place and leaves you with a lasting memory. Isn't that what tea has been doing for centuries?

Touring suggestions: Tea lovers visiting Epcot will not want to miss The Tea Caddy, located in the UK section. You can buy teas and gifts or enjoy iced tea from the tea bar before stepping into the Twinings Garden to discover the history of Twinings tea.

THE DRAKE HOTEL

Chicago, Illinois

The familiar strains of "As Time Goes By" drift from the harp and across the room as guests sip tea in the low light of The Palm Court. The palatial setting is only steps away from one of the world's busiest shopping districts, Michigan Avenue's Magnificent Mile. Time does "go by" here, just a little bit slower than the rest of the bustling city.

Located in the grand Drake Hotel, business travelers, families on vacation, tired shoppers, and old friends know this as the ideal spot for an sophisticated afternoon retreat.

Chicagoans often choose this quiet room to commemorate the passing of time. Celebrations regularly unfold here. Young girls enjoying a birthday or couples seated cozily in a quiet corner toasting an anniversary are frequent scenes here. This is a place where memories are made.

The classic 13-story hotel with its mammoth rooftop sign has been an icon on Chicago's famous lakefront since opening in 1921. Built by brothers John and Tracy Drake, the National Registry landmark has hosted numerous world leaders from Emperor Hirohito of Japan to Queen Elizabeth II of England. It has been completely restored under the management of Hilton Hotels.

Located off the main lobby and up a short wide flight of stairs, the opulent Palm Court is filled with marble-topped tables, cushioned loveseats, and arm chairs set among Chinese lacquered screens and, of course, potted palms. A fantastic crystal chandelier casts a golden light across the room that is reflected in the mirrored columns and ceiling. The harpist is strategically placed at the top of the stairs so that her music mystically lures lobby guests out of the mundane and into this heavenly setting.

The centerpiece of the Palm Court is a fabulous antique urn fountain in the center of the room. Stone cherubs and dolphins frolic around its enormous floral arrangement. The urn looks as if it has always been a part of the Palm Court environment, but the 270-year old antique was purchased from a New York garden sculpture house twenty years ago. The room was redesigned around it. The floral print fabrics on the couches, the greenery, the custom built fountain base and the lobby appointments were all hand picked to create a proper setting for the baroque urn.

What better way to showcase the relaxing elegance of the room than with a proper afternoon tea? The tea choices include standard selections of English Breakfast, Earl Grey, Darjeeling and Irish

enough to spend more time exploring the superb cultural opportunities that await you in this world class city.

The Drake has naturally become a regular stop for returning visitors. It easy to see why this legendary landmark has become an established old friend to so many.

Touring suggestions: Downtown Chicago is one of the world's easiest big cities to navigate. With a convenient subway and commuter train route, you can be anywhere in a matter of minutes. It's a great walking city.

Before setting out on foot, consider starting with an overview of the city. The Sears Tower Skydeck and John Hancock Observatory offer sweeping vistas from 1000 feet above ground level. Next, consider a visit to historic Navy Pier. Beautifully perched on Lake Michigan, Navy Pier features the 50,000-square-foot Chicago Children's Museum,

Blend with the interesting addition of herbal infusions such as Honeybush, Wild Blossoms and Berries, Chamomile Citrus, and flavored teas such as Bombay Chai and Chocolate Mint Truffle. The tea is served English style with the tea leaves remaining in the pot. Attentive servers keep the hot water refreshed.

The three-tiered tray arrives bearing four nicely trimmed tea sandwiches: tomato and cucumber, beef with onion, egg salad, and asparagus rolls. Scones with whipped cream and preserves accompany these. These round yeast scones are more like a bun than a traditional English scone.

Topping off the afternoon is an assortment of pastries including a chocolate torte, lemon square, Napoleon, and fresh fruit tart. Champagne is an option for your special occasion.

The Drake also caters to children by offering child friendly tea foods at a reduced price.

The Palm Court's sophisticated and refreshing respite will undoubtedly renew your energy

a 440-seat IMAX Theatre, and is home to 40,000 square feet of exciting restaurants and retail shops, live music, and more. Just beyond, discover the Crystal Gardens, a 32,000-square-foot indoor botanical park. A variety of boat tours depart from Navy Pier and other city locations, as well as city bus tours, which point out significant landmarks and provide interesting information about Chicago and its history.

No visit to The Windy City is complete without a visit to the Art Institute of Chicago. It's home to one of the great collections of Impressionist art. Across the street you'll find Russian Tea Time, another exotic location for afternoon tea.

The Museum Campus, near Soldier Field, is home to the Field Museum of Natural History and the Adler Planetarium, two excellent museums. Also located at Museum Campus is the Shedd Aquarium, the world's largest indoor aquarium with more than 8,000 aquatic animals representing more than 700 species from all parts of the world.

For an unforgettable shopping and entertainment experience, be sure to walk Chicago's Magnificent Mile, Michigan Avenue. With four shopping centers, world-renowned boutiques, locally acclaimed designers, and lovely streetside gardens throughout, this area simply cannot be missed. In addition to extensive shopping and sightseeing opportunities, there is a wealth of architectural masterpieces along the avenue.

Be sure to check out the exterior of the Chicago Tribune Building. Its walls are filled with fascinating souvenir stones scavenged from many of the world's most famous historic sites.

Another interesting neighborhood lies across Michigan Avenue from the Drake. Take a walk along Oak Street and window shop through the unending collection of boutiques and outdoor cafes. It's less congested and a bit more relaxed than Michigan Avenue. For an evening of theatre, continue on to the Steppenwolf Theatre, one of the best regional stages in America.

DUNBAR TEA ROOM

Sandwich, Massachusettes

No visit to Massachusetts is complete without a visit to Cape Cod. Here lies one of America's great collections of early American villages, homes, shops, lighthouses and pristine beaches. Postcard perfect vistas await you around every turn. Town after town contains white-spire churches and weathered salt box homes. Antique shops spill their wares onto the sidewalks and lovingly restored bed & breakfast inns welcome visitors from around the world. One of the oldest and most picturesque towns on the northern coast is also one of the most accessible.

Founded in 1637, Sandwich became the site of one of America's largest glass factories during the 19th century. The town also was the home of Thornton Burgess, author of Peter Cottontail. Here, too, stands the First Church of Christ. Built in 1830, it has a spire designed by noted English architect Christopher Wren. It is one of the most photographed buildings on the cape.

Across the street is the Dexter Grist Mill (dating from the 1640's) where you can see Leo the Miller grinding his corn. Next door is the Thornton Burgess Museum. Just up the street, the Hoxie House, one of the oldest houses on Cape Cod (1675) is furnished with period pieces. Around the corner is Yesteryear's Doll Museum housing an extensive collection of rare and antique dolls.

One of New England's best tea rooms lies in the heart of Sandwich, within the shadow of Christopher Wren's church spire. Since opening in 1991, the Dunbar Tea Shop has been featured in many guides, newspapers and magazines from around the world, including *The Boston Globe, The Cape Cod Times, The Washington Post, Yankee Magazine, National Geographic Traveler Magazine, Cape Cod Life, Travel Magazine, Fodor's,* and *Frommer's.*

Tea is served in the former Carriage House, located to the right of the main 1740 house where owners Paula and Jim Hegarty reside. The main dining room sits in an old wood paneled gentlemen's smoking and billiard room.

Now it is home to the clinking of teacups rather than billiard balls, and the air is filled with the aroma of baking pies, cakes, shortbreads and scones rather than pipe smoke. The tea room has a warm fireplace to fight the chill of stiff winter winds. Talk about cozy! The intimate room seats no more than 25 people so you feel as if you are having tea in an English home. In the summer, additional seating

for 30 diners is available on the patio or in a shady tea garden.

The Tea Shop has become an unique institution and an integral part of a trip to Sandwich. The Hegarty's have developed a great reputation over the years for homemade goods, a wide selection of brewed loose teas and an innovative menu.

Anyone who has traveled to the British Isles will feel right at home with a menu featuring such favorites as a Ploughman's Lunch, Smoked Scottish Salmon Platter, Cumberland Crumpet Melt, petticoat shortbread and, of course, scones with jam and cream. Tea is made British style - loose tea in the pot with a silver strainer. There are all the traditional favorites amongst the fourteen tea offerings. Cozies keep the tea piping hot once it reaches your table.

The Windsor Afternoon Tea comes with all the expected courses: scones with jam and cream, dessert bars, and assorted finger sandwiches. The menu changes seasonally.

Guests need to pace themselves so that they save room for a slice of one of the cakes or pies displayed on the buffet. One of the favorites is the Princess Cake composed of three layers of pound cake with raspberry filling and almond cream frosting. Portions are huge and most customers are seen leaving with a box of leftovers to enjoy at home.

The gift shop is tea heaven filled to the brim with every tea item available. Shelves of teapots, cozies, tea strainers and teacups are all there to help you recreate the perfect Dunbar Tea Shop experience at home.

Excited shoppers can be heard exclaiming "Oh, your sister would love this!" or "I haven't seen one of these since I was in Cornwall." It's a great place to explore while you wait for your table. Adding to the Anglomania is a complete selection of imported British foods that can satisfy any ex-patriot's yearning for such homeland staples as PG Tips or Marmite.

The Hegartys have found an unbeaten way to make a visit to Cape Cod a deliciously satisfying experience. Their tea shop wonderland has successfully blended the best of old England with the best of New England.

Forget about Boston. The real tea party is here in Sandwich!

Touring suggestions: One of the biggest attractions on the western cape is the Sandwich Glass Museum and its world class collection of exhibits. The Museum tells the story of a Massachusetts farming community and of Deming Jarves, an entrepreneur from Boston. It is the story of America's decorative glass industry at the dawn of the Industrial Revolution and one of the greatest glass factories, the Boston & Sandwich Glass Company.

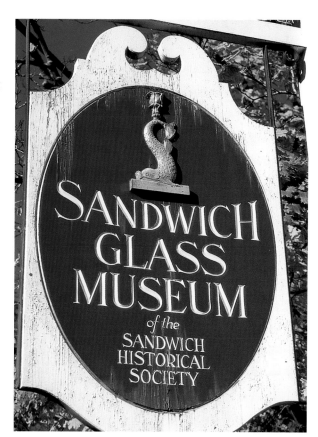

Fourteen galleries house over 5,000 glass creations on display. Don't miss the extensive collection of pressed glass cup holders. These souvenirs were all the rage a century and a half ago when hot tea was poured into the saucer in order for it to cool. The tea was often drunk directly from the saucer. The teacup had to be placed somewhere while the both hands were used to lift the saucer. The cup plate was invented to protect furniture from the teacup rings that might come from placing a cup on bare furniture and an industry was born.

Sandwich also has a number of interesting shops, ranging from a weather store to antique emporia. Visitors often take an afternoon stroll up Grove Street past some grand colonials and the old town burial ground (some grave stones date from the 17th century) to the Heritage Plantation.

The plantation's 100 acres of beautifully landscaped grounds are home to a spectacular rhododendron blossom in May & June. The grounds are a naturalized woodland park on the edge of upper Shawme Pond. There's even an operating Dutch windmill on the ground. A Shaker round barn houses an antique automobile collection and The American History Museum displays an operating hand-carved carousel and works by many of America's most distinguished artists. Don't miss the rare shell-covered labyrinth hidden in a cove of trees.

Another stop on most itineraries is the Daniel Webster Inn on Main Street. An inn has stood on this spot for over three centuries. Called the Fessenden Tavern from the mid 1700s until the 1800s, the tavern's most notable visitor was Daniel Webster, one of the most prominent men of his day. He had a room reserved at the tavern from 1815 to 1851.

DUSHANBE TEAHOUSE

Boulder, Colorado

Taking tea with friends has been a unifying experience for thousands of years. Nowhere is the convivial custom more evident than in the Rocky Mountains north of Denver. The sister cities of Boulder, Colorado and Dushanbe, Tajikistan have taken the art and camaraderie of tea to its highest level.

In 1987, during his first visit to Boulder, Dushanbe's Mayor Maksud Ikramov announced that he planned to present the city with a teahouse to celebrate the establishment of sister city ties. Dushanbe {doo-shan-bay} is the capital of Tajikistan. The name, meaning "Monday," is derived from the day of the week on which a bazaar was held in the village.

Using skills handed down from generation to generation, more than 40 artisans in several cities of Tajikistan created the decorative elements for the teahouse, including its hand-carved and hand-painted ceiling, tables, stools, columns, and exterior ceramic panels.

In central Asia, teahouses serve as gathering places where friends meet to talk or play chess over a cup of tea. Many teahouses are traditionally decorated with lavish Persian art, characterized by the use of motifs from nature - stellar, solar, and floral. The Dushanbe Teahouse accurately reflects this artistic tradition dating back nearly 2,000 years. The master

woodcarvers who helped reassemble the teahouse here have carved their names into the ceiling. The artisans who painted it have written their names on a green painted area above the entry to the kitchen. A message carved into the ceiling reads "artisans of ancient Khojand whose works are magical."

A magical place it is! The aroma of curry and other exotic spices greets guests as they enter. Although tables fill the restaurant, many of the best seats are topjans (raised wooden platforms with cushions). Where else in this hemisphere can you experience the ritual of tea as you sit on pillows? Take your shoes off and sip a cup of hot aromatic chai tea. You will be dining like Alexander the Great because the topjans recall the teahouse's central Asian roots where guests are invited to recline for their tea, as in a Bedouin tent. The center of the room is dominated by a central pool surrounded by seven hammered copper sculptures created by artist Ivan Milosovich. The life sized feminine images are based on a 12th century poem, "The Seven Beauties."

The ceiling of the teahouse was carved and painted with intricate traditional Persian art patterns. The ceiling was originally built, carved and painted in Tajikistan. Absolutely no power tools were used in the original construction. The work

Reservations are required for this luxurious tea time in Boulder's most exotic atmosphere.

The teahouse sits just off Central Park in downtown Boulder, nestled against the majestic Flatirons Mountains. Each weekend, the Boulder County Farmer's Market is set up on the street in front of the teahouse, offering a colorful display of vegetables and crafts to passers-by.

Sara is a master at creating children's tea events. What better location could there be for a child's birthday party with an international theme?

was crafted by hand, exactly as it was centuries ago. Inside the teahouse, there are 12 intricately carved cedar columns. No two columns are alike.

Eight colorful ceramic panels, created by Victor Zabolotnikov, grace the building's exterior and display patterns of a "Tree of Life." Each panel was sculpted in Tajikistan, cut into smaller tiles, fired, and then carefully packed to be sent to Boulder. Once here, they were repositioned by the artist.

The teahouse offers an eclectic mix of dishes from around the world with an emphasis on traditional Tajik and Persian entrees such as Lamb Shish Kabob, Tajik Plov, and Persian Vegetarian Kooftah Balls. Owners Sara and Lennie Martinelli have expertly composed both the menu and tea list that contains 80-90 exquisite choices sourced from tea growing regions around the world.

A traditional afternoon tea is served on white linen with an assortment of pastries and sweets, scones with cream and lemon curd, tea sandwiches, and a choice of brewed teas served in Chatsford pots.

Touring suggestions: Anyone who appreciates tea will want to visit the nearby Celestial Seasonings factory, appropriately located at the edge of town on Sleepy Time Lane. The free hour-long tour begins in a sampling room where guests taste hot or cold teas and then record their tea reviews. An informative video gives everyone a history of the colorful Boulder industry that now produces over a million teabags each day.

The leisurely tour through the working area of the plant is highlighted by stepping into the eye-opening peppermint vault and a fascinating view of the blending and packaging areas. A well-stocked tea gift shop caps the event.

Boulder is filled with highly educated, active people who are constantly striving for a healthy lifestyle. Cyclists and hikers are in abundance in this outdoor paradise.

The front range of the Rocky Mountains rise to the west of Boulder. An hour north lies the village of Estes Park, gateway to Rocky Mountain National Park and Roosevelt National Forest. This is an outdoor oasis filled with spectacular mountain scenery, abundant wildlife habitat, miles of hiking trails and scenic drives including Trail Ridge Road over the Continental Divide and the Peak to Peak Scenic Byway.

While the weather in Boulder is mostly sunny and dry, a late afternoon thunderstorm is almost a daily occurrence on the high mountain trails. Be sure to set out early and arrive back before mid afternoon.

A drive south from Boulder leads to the old west town of Golden. You may stop by the Briarwood Inn for a classic afternoon tea in a beautiful setting or continue on to Denver for a lobby tea at the historic Brown Palace.

These tea experiences in the Boulder area are unlike anything you will find in America. A trip to this open-minded college town at the base of the Rocky Mountains gives you new insight into the international flavor of tea.

THE FAIRMONT CHATEAU LAKE LOUISE

Lake Louise, Alberta

The pristine Banff National Park has earned the reputation of being known as "Canada's Diamond in the Wilderness," and the "Hiking Capital of Canada." This wilderness area offers a tremendous diversity of recreational and sightseeing opportunities. None is more breathtaking than Lake Louise.

This mountain hideaway is home to one of North America's finest downhill ski areas and has numerous hiking and walking trails. Those trails abound with spectacular vistas, from glaciers to waterfalls.

Tea has been an important part of the daily ritual in this mountaintop wonderland since 1883, when the transcontinental railway reached the formidable Rocky Mountains. The discovery of natural hot springs bubbling from the base of Sulphur Mountain led to the establishment of Canada's first national park, Rocky Mountain Park. Early park rangers stashed their tea and equipage in bear proof tins along the rugged trails so they could enjoy a hot cup of tea when working on the coldest of days.

Today, Banff National Park is one of four adjoining mountain parks comprising more than 5,200 square miles of spectacular Canadian Rocky Mountain landscape. Each year, four million international visitors soak in the warm water of the springs and soak up the uninterrupted natural beauty of this world heritage site.

The man-made crown jewel of the park is The Fairmont Chateau Lake Louise. It was constructed over a century ago as part of the Canadian Pacific Railway's "ribbon of steel," built to link Canada's populated centers with the vast potential of its relatively unpopulated West. William Cornelius VanHorne, general manager of Canadian Pacific Railway was often quoted as saying, "Since we can't export the scenery, we'll have to import the tourists."

He built sixteen fantastic European-inspired palaces that attracted countless well-to-do tourists who traveled in plush railway coaches from one beautiful chateau to another until they finally reached the grand Empress Hotel in Victoria, British Columbia.

The Fairmont Chateau Lake Louise sits on the shore of the azure-blue Lake Louise, 50 minutes north of Banff Springs. The picture postcard setting is perfectly framed with emerald green forests and snow-capped mountains that glisten under a dramatic Canadian sky.

The villa designs of the Italian Renaissance influenced the architecture of this chateau that once served as a hideaway for Fairbanks and Barrymore, Monroe and Hitchcock. Residents can spend the day skiing, fly-fishing, hiking, canoeing, or simply reading a book while tucked away in one of the second-floor alcoves.

The selection of teas are specially blended for the Fairmont chain of resorts and hotels. Highlighting the traditional selection of teas is the Fairmont Blend and other traditional teas blended by Canada's Metropolitan Tea Company. It's evident that this hotel is serious about tea. Not only do they have their own signature blends, but, in addition, each guest suite has its own hot water kettle and a selection of teas to enjoy throughout your stay.

The pampering goes on and on at tea time. An optional flute of Champagne tops off your afternoon with one more bit of sparkle. It's hard to imagine a more relaxing way to spend a couple of hours. This is a memory that won't soon be forgotten. You better ask someone to photograph you here so you can show your friends how perfect this setting is. Mere words won't do it justice.

There is just one problem: you won't want to leave this sunny setting where staring out the window is relaxing and encouraged.

The highlight of the day for tea lovers is Afternoon Tea in the Lakeview Lounge. Tea time settings don't get much more spectacular than the snow-capped scenery outside the windows. The preferred tables for two are located by Palladian windows that allow an uninterrupted alpine-like view of the lake and mountains.

The only temptations that draw your attention from this stunning natural vista are the beautiful handmade savories and decadent sweets designed by the hotel's chefs.

Afternoon Tea begins with a refreshing compote of fresh fruit. A tiered server is soon presented, bearing a colorful array of tea sandwiches—cucumber, smoked salmon, egg on wheat, and chicken with mango pinwheels.

Perfect English scones are served with a generous supply of clotted cream and preserves. Other tantalizing sweets include miniature éclairs, custard tarts, handmade chocolates, and shortbreads crowned with whole strawberries.

Touring suggestions: The mountains framing Lake Louise are crisscrossed with hiking trails. One of the favorite routes is the Lake Agnes Trail that begins at the rear of the hotel and climbs 1,000 feet to glacier-fed Lake Agnes.

A 90-minute walk will bring you to a glorious tea respite, probably unlike any you have seen. The Lake Agnes log chalet teahouse, circa 1900, hugs the shore of this emerald lake. But be warned. This is not a tea room for hats and lace gloves. There is no electricity. The chalet is warmed by a wood stove and lit by kerosene lamps. In fact, this may be the only tea room you have visited that has an outhouse. There is seating for about 15 guests indoors, and there are several rustic tables lining the front porch where tea may be enjoyed on warmer days.

Owner Cynthia Magee rebuilt the teahouse after purchasing it from the Canadian Pacific Railway in 1981. It is so remote that supplies are brought in by helicopters or horseback, and her hardworking staff lives onsite in another small cabin.

The simple menu includes soup, sandwiches, tea biscuits, and homemade pastries. Most amazing about this sanctuary is its assortment of fifty loose teas from all over the world. Tea never tasted as good—or as warming—as when you cradle the steaming cup on a snowy fall afternoon. Thinking about all the effort that went into getting your tea to this outpost, you don't want to waste a drop.

Tea water is heated in six huge kettles that continually simmer on a mammoth gas stove in the kitchen. (It takes a lot of heat to boil water at an elevation of 8,000 feet.)

The trek to Lake Agnes can be exhausting, and more than a few out-of-breath adventurers turn back to the comfort of their hotel rooms. But they miss the reward that lies at the end of the journey. Those who persevere will have an incredible story—and photographs—to share with tea friends back home.

It's hard to image a setting where tea is more "high" than this mountaintop Shangri-La.

THE FAIRMONT EMPRESS HOTEL

Victoria, British Columbia

There is a bit of Britain nestled beside a rugged bay on an enchanted island in the southwest corner of British Columbia where the gentle custom of afternoon tea is still celebrated in grand style. "More English than the English" was true of the first English-born Victorians who established Fort Victoria in 1843, seeking to create a society based on a nostalgic, half-remembered homeland. Today the city of Victoria has grown into one of the top urban destinations for world travelers. At the city's heart, welcoming guests as they arrive by boat or ferry, is the magnificent Fairmont Empress Hotel.

Since its opening in 1908, the hotel has long been accustomed to entertaining Hollywood celebrities. Rita Hayworth, Jack Benny, Pat O'Brien, Douglas Fairbanks, Katherine Hepburn, Bob Hope, Bing Crosby, Tallulah Bankhead, Roger Moore, John Travolta, Barbara Streisand, Harrison Ford and a host of others have passed through its lobby. Shirley Temple arrived accompanied by her parents amid rumors that she had fled from California because of kidnapping threats, a story born from the presence of two huge bodyguards who took the room opposite hers and always left their door open.

By 1965, there was much debate on whether to tear down what was becoming a faded, dowdy hotel, to make room for a more modern, functional high-rise hotel. One local newspaper warned that, "Without this splendid relic of the Edwardian era, literally tens of thousands of tourists will never return. This is the Mecca, this is the heart and soul of the city."

The decision was announced on June 10, 1966: The Fairmont Empress would not be demolished. Instead she would embark on a $4 million campaign of renovation and refurbishment, playfully dubbed "Operation Teacup."

Stories of unusual guests and employees abound. In 1987, a woman wrote about her wonderful stay at The Fairmont Empress and asked if other guests had received a similar late night visitor - a little girl who had watched over her bed and then floated across the room. There also are the stories of an early 20th century maid, who appears now and then on the sixth floor to help with the cleaning.

In 1989, over $45 million was spent on the royal restoration. All guest rooms were renovated, and a health club, indoor swimming pool and guest reception were added. With an emphasis on craftsmanship, no attempt was made to give the hotel a new image. Instead, the goal was to restore The Empress to her original elegance.

The strong emotions The Fairmont Empress evokes in many of her guests and protectors is exemplified in the statement made by an irate gentleman, as workers raised the sign above the front entrance, "Anyone who doesn't know this is The Empress shouldn't be staying here."

Afternoon tea is what you do when you visit Victoria. And nowhere is this daily celebration observed more royally than in the opulent hotel. In all of North America, there is not a tea venue which has introduced more guests to the pleasures of afternoon tea. Each year thousands of people enjoy this beloved pastime that has unfolded daily with great ceremony since the hotel opened.

Guests are invited to sip tea and enjoy delicious food and pleasant conversation accompanied by the relaxing music of a string quartet while seated in the famous Tea Lobby. The rose and green-trimmed lobby ceiling is over 15 feet high and supports 12 original chandeliers. A pair of period George V and Queen Mary portraits stand watch over the matching

fireplaces. Tea patrons are seated at comfortable couches or chintz-covered high-back chairs set before antique wooden tea tables.

Summertime guests may take their tea at wicker tables along the verandah and watch boats arriving in the harbor, just as travelers have done for nearly a century. This same small port once welcomed fast-sailing clipper ships laden with tea imported for a growing population of tea-drinking British colonists and Chinese laborers.

In cooler months, a leisurely tea at the Empress begins with a mild shrimp pâté and crackers. Fresh fruit with chantilly cream is offered in season. The Tea at The Empress blend is a selection of seasonal, quality teas, created exclusively for The Fairmont Empress. This classic blend of Assam, Kenyan, Nilgiri, Ceylon, and Chinese black teas is the perfect accompaniment for any elegant afternoon tea presented in the British fashion. A box of this signature blend makes a prized souvenir of your visit.

The highlight of the meal is the arrival of a three-tiered server laden with traditional tea sandwiches such as smoked salmon, sliced cucumber, carrot and ginger with cream cheese, pesto egg salad on foccacia

crostini, and curry mango chicken salad. Of course, no tea is complete without raisin scones accompanied by clotted cream and strawberry preserves. The chefs here have quite a bit of experience in producing these delicious creations.

Perched temptingly on top of the silver server are delicate bite-size pastries, including caramel chocolate truffles in chocolate cups, lemon curd tarts with glazed berries, choux pastries filled with green tea white chocolate cream, sour cherry almond pound cakes, and traditional shortbread cookies. It's more than enough to sustain you through an afternoon of touring and walking through flower gardens.

The Fairmont Empress is not content to rest on its laurels. In a world where tea drinkers are becoming more and more sophisticated, this jewel in the Canadian Pacific crown has quite a reputation to maintain. Luckily for visitors to this paradise, the afternoon tea has been, and will continue to be, one of the unforgettable memories delighted visitors carry back to the real world.

Touring suggestions: A great way to walk off those clotted cream calories is to wander through the variety of fascinating shops that line nearby Government Street. Victoria's British heritage is apparent in the store windows which display woolens and bone china from England, tartans from Scotland and Irish lace. Stop to sample handmade chocolates or another perfect cup of tea. Native art, jewelry, fashion, and souvenir shops also abound.

Four blocks along Government Street, turn right into Trounce Alley, one of Victoria's best-kept secrets. European fashions and gift shops await. Just beyond Bastion Square, turn left off Government Street onto Johnson. Wander among heritage buildings restored to maintain an old-town ambience and visit Market Square with over 40 merchants and eateries.

Victoria's city layout is ideal for walking. Historic government buildings, flower baskets hanging from lampposts, harbor views and mountain scenery entice visitors down cobblestone sidewalks and pedestrian-friendly walkways to a world of discoveries.

GRAND AMERICAN HOTEL

Salt Lake City, Utah

The Grand American Hotel lies between the desolate splendor of the Great Salt Lake and a backdrop of alpine crags forming the Wasatch Mountains. The 24-story hotel rises from the desert floor like a grand gateway to the wide avenues leading through the historic business district of downtown Salt Lake City and the soaring spires and gilded angels of Temple Square.

Built by the Sinclair Oil Corporation just in time for the 2002 Winter Olympics, this hotel is indeed "grand" in every sense of the word. Inspired by the charm and craftsmanship of Europe's classic hotels, the Grand America offers 775 luxurious rooms and covers 10 acres of beautifully landscaped grounds. Murano crystal chandeliers, handcrafted Richelieu furniture, English wool carpets, Carrara Italian marble, original oil paintings, and luxurious fabrics give a refined sense reminiscent of entering a European castle. Guests might find it hard to believe that they are still in the rugged American West.

No great European style hotel is complete without a proper afternoon tea. The Grand American showcases their tea service front and center in the elegantly sophisticated Lobby Lounge. The strains of an angelic harp and a spectacular view of the garden courtyard lure you into this sophisticated retreat. A massive fireplace adds a comfortable warm touch and takes the chill out of tea drinking skiers who have spent the morning on nearby slopes. Guests are further enticed by a dessert trolley filled to overflowing with handcrafted pastries, cakes, and gateaux.

The "Grand Traditions Tea" begins with a glass of Champagne and continues with a selection of domestic and imported cheeses, seasonal fruit, and a delightful array of delicious finger sandwiches that include prosciutto, pacific cold smoked salmon, and bay shrimp salad with watercress. English scones are accompanied by rich Devonshire Cream and strawberry jam.

The grand finale is an assortment of freshly made tea pastries and cakes taken from the dessert trolley you have been eyeing all afternoon. A complete selection of 25 loose teas includes all the standard selections as well as Cranberry Autumn, Chocolate Mint, Tropical Green, Spiced Plum and French Verveine.

This delicious atmosphere is conducive to conversation as well. There is never a hurried moment or a sense of time passing here. This is a room intended to pamper all the senses. The hotel's moniker truly is "see how much delight is possible in a single afternoon."

system based on the four streets bordering Temple Square, the focus of the downtown area. Inside Temple Square is the Mormon Temple, which took 40 years to build—from 1853 to 1893. New brides and grooms can often be seen entering the Temple. The Thursday evening Mormon Tabernacle Choir rehearsals are open to the public and a free half-hour organ recital is given weekdays at noon. Both are held in the nearby Mormon Conference Center.

Salt Lake combines the amenities of a large metro area with the opportunity to take advantage of year round outdoor recreation within minutes in every direction. An attractive, safe, and growing city, Salt Lake offers unequaled mountain scenery, a thriving economy, remarkable history and the warm hospitality of a small western town. The performing arts are alive with Ballet West, Utah Opera Company, and The Utah Symphony. Numerous theater groups and over twenty art galleries are within minutes of The Grand American Hotel.

Touring Suggestions: Since hosting the 2002 Winter Olympic Games, Salt Lake City has continued to put a shine on its image and showcase the city's reputation as a prime destination for visitors from around the world. When winter hits, the snow falls on the slopes of four nearby ski resorts: Alta, Brighton, Snowbird, and Solitude. Park City, home of Utah Olympic Park, is less than a 40 minute drive from downtown Salt Lake. From Park City, you may continue on a loop to Sundance and the panoramic vistas surrounding Provo before returning to Salt Lake City.

Downtown Salt Lake City is noted for its wide streets and spacious blocks, a legacy of the Mormon settlers who laid out the city in 1847. Be warned. A city block here is twice as long as in most cities and comfortable walking shoes are recommended for afternoon or evening strolls. Fortunately, the city's transit system (TRAX) has a stop close to The Grand American. The city was built on a grid

LADY MENDL'S

New York, New York

Manhattan Island's early Dutch residents possessed an unquenchable thirst for tea. Early New Yorkers loved tea so much that they erected several "tea water pumps" over fresh water springs in lower Manhattan. The clear, bubbling water kept the kitchen kettles full. The springs were located in the vicinity of Christopher Street and at Fourteenth Street and Tenth Avenue. The more affluent residents depended upon peddlers of tea-water who paraded their carts along the cobbled streets supplying the precious liquid to kitchen kettles as far north as mid-Manhattan.

The colonists' desire for the precious beverage and King George's subsequent taxes eventually caused the colonials to break their bonds with the British monarchy and sign a pledge to forgo their daily cup of tea. Three hundred years later, tea is drawing people into this area of Manhattan again.

Gramercy Park is one of four squares laid out by real estate developers in the 19th century to emulate the quiet, private residential areas in many European cities. The townhouses around the square were designed by some of the city's best architects and occupied by its most prominent citizens. Teddy Roosevelt was born just a block away on East 20th Street. Exclusive residences and clubs remain around New York's last private park.

Only those who live on the square have an entrance key to the fenced oasis. But, all can enjoy the peace and charm of the area around it.

A stroll south from the park, down Irving Place, leads to East 19th Street, known as "The Block Beautiful." This handsome tree-lined stretch of restored 1920 residences is a block from Pete's Tavern. Since 1903, this cozy neighborhood pub has welcomed thirsty guests, including O. Henry who wrote *The Gift of the Magi* in the second booth.

The next block is home to one of New York's premier boutique hotels and tea rooms, The Inn at Irving Place and Lady Mendl's Tea Salon.

Guests have to look closely for the location. The name is not posted on the townhouse and only a discreet brass plaque bears the name "Lady Mendl's." Its quiet anonymity is what brings many of its customers and celebrity guests back again and again.

Two 1834 landmark townhouses have been meticulously transformed to recreate a bygone era of gracious living. The 12 guest rooms and suites are furnished with exquisite antiques reminiscent of Edith Wharton's New York. Each room bears the name of an interesting local personality from the early 20th century Gramercy Park neighborhood.

Lady Mendl's Tea Salon is named for Elsie DeWolfe, a flamboyant socialite and designer who once lived

wiches that include smoked salmon with crème fraiche, cucumber with creamery butter, goat cheese with sundried tomato, and smoked turkey and cranberry on brioche.

In true afternoon tea fashion, scones with Devonshire cream and preserves come next. The dessert course consists of several tempting cakes - chocolate, lemon, or carrot, to name a few. The meal ends with a selection of beautiful cookies and chocolate covered strawberries. The service is efficient without being pretentious and the wait staff anticipates every need.

Afternoon tea at Lady Mendl's is a memorable event. The sophisticated and leisurely meal is never rushed.

These are comfortable rooms reminiscent of a quiet Parisian boutique hotel where old friends chat for hours and couples, caught in the sweetness of the moment, lose track of time. After all, it is difficult to think about looking at your watch while cradling a warm cup of Darjeeling in your hands.

across the street. She married Lord Mendl, giving her the convenient title of Lady Mendl. She loved tea but not the Victorian fluff that went with it. She was known for bringing homes up-to-date by tearing off heavy Victorian wallpapers and covering walls with the clean look of paint.

Lady Mendl's has a romantic old-world atmosphere. The tall first floor rooms are lit by antique lamps, classic chandeliers, and soft sunlight filtering through the wood-shuttered windows. Small, intimate tables are scattered throughout the two rooms. Guests may sit at sofas placed before the fireplace on a winter day. Several tables may be joined to accommodate larger parties.

This is one of New York's most fashionable settings for a bridal tea, and the tea rooms are often booked months in advance. Another private dining room is located just behind the registration area for these special events.

The five-course Lady Mendl's Royal Tea begins with a light salad followed by a quartet of tea sand-

MISS MABLE'S

Dickson, Tennessee

Open the door to any successful tea room and you're likely to find an owner with great passion and an unending desire to offer warm hospitality and outstanding service. Miss Mable's Tea Room in Dickson, Tennessee, is a shining example of why Americans are returning to tea rooms and tea shops in growing numbers.

Who's the driving force behind this wildly successful business that draws customers from all over the greater Nashville area?

Fay Davidson started looking for a site in 1994. Her goal was to have a place where women could gather and relax around a cup of tea. She did her homework by attending professional seminars on beginning a tea business.

Fay was drawn to a neglected West College Street neighborhood that needed attention. After restoring a building for a gift shop and calling it Nana's Attic, she set her sights on a vacant 100-year-old house sitting across the street, the ideal setting for the tea room. It would be a year before Fay and her husband, Mark, would finish the extensive renovations needed to bring the neglected building back to its original design and decor. With the entire family's assistance, the goal was accomplished, and the tea room and gift shop began drawing customers from all over the southeastern region of the United States.

Inspiration came from the life of Fay's grandmother, affectionately called Miss Mable, who raised 13 children in the Dickson community. Family tradition said that Mable stood for "Mothers Always Bring a Loving Experience."

Guests first notice the enticing southern porch that wraps around the house. It is filled with white wicker furniture and floral cushions, the perfect retreat for tea guests in the spring before the oppressive heat that accompanies a Tennessee summer. In the driveway sits Miss Mable's PT Cruiser with the inscription "Driving Miss Mable" across the back. On its roof is a gigantic fiberglass red hat, a lure to the countless Red Hat Societies that come calling.

Inside, the decor is an unapologetic combination of Victorian kitsch and southern charm – Grandmother's attic in the best sense. This tea room is a nostalgic playhouse where women may don any of the 400 hats, shawls, or lace gloves covering the walls and chair backs. Lace-covered tables hold mismatched china teacups and silver tea strainers. Boldly patterned wallpaper, antique tables and sideboards, lamps with frilly shades, and tasseled curtains add to the dramatic setting, where patrons become actresses in a play that unfolds throughout the week. It is a place where you could easily lose track of time.

extensive list of 62 teas before the parade of delicious food arrives displayed on tiered servers, glass dishes and silver trays. Each item is beautifully prepared and presented. Guests feel as if they are having tea in a friend's home.

Fay Davidson has created the perfect southern tea room in an area that loves nostalgic memories of a slower life and simpler times. She has honored the memory of her grandmother by "Always Bringing Loving Experiences" to the guests who enter. Mable would be proud.

Decorator items, tea accoutrements, and fashions needed for an at-home tea party are scattered throughout the four tea rooms and the second floor gift shops. It is a wonderland that cannot be fully appreciated with just one visit. Guests come back again and again.

Fay counts herself fortunate in having a supportive family that works behind the scenes to make Miss Mable's flourish. Sons Joseph and John Michael both help out while her daughter Jennifer helps manage the tea room. Jennifer's husband, Chuck Jones, is the head chef.

Chuck's well-equipped kitchen turns out beautiful soups, quiches, buttermilk scones, shrimp salads, tea sandwiches, and a tempting array of desserts that constantly changes. His signature creme bruleè in a demitasse cup is a traditional favorite.

The afternoon tea menu varies monthly with different themes such as a Gone with the Wind Tea or a Rose Garden Tea. Customers choose from the

QUEEN MARY TEA ROOM

Seattle, Washington

Seattle is a town that sees a lot of overcast days. Dark gray clouds, laden with warm Pacific moisture, blow in regularly from the west and drop their burdens on the rich green landscape. Generous rain is great for the profuse flora that thrives in this moisture-rich environment, but the lack of sunshine can take its toll on the inhabitants of this sun-deprived corner of Washington. Residents long for a reprieve from the overcast skies and a comforting dose of hot tea to carry them to the next ray of sunshine.

Since 1988, the tea drinking populace of Seattle has turned to an ivy-covered, English-style tea room for a bit of solace and a generous helping of British comfort food. Whether they come for a hearty breakfast of Bangers and Mash with a pot of English Breakfast, or the full Royal Afternoon Tea with a flute of Kir Royale, each customer of The Queen Mary Tea Room is given a royal welcome by the owner Mary Greengo.

Mary has always had a reputation for looking after details. One envious friend once commented "Who do you think you are? Queen Mary?" The name was too good to let go, and Mary claimed the moniker as the title for her restaurant that sits along an inclined street, 10 blocks north of the University of Washington.

Brightly waving banners and overflowing flower boxes beckon guests as they approach the regal red door. To the left of the front door, Mary's royal birds, Princess and Angel, coo to all who pass by. The door opens to an eye-popping shop filled with every imaginable tea gift and accoutrement.

Glittering delights are stacked to the ceiling in an overwhelming display of tea temptations. This is an Anglophile's dream. There is even a pastry case as you enter, stocked with tea cakes, trifles, and Devon double cream so that you can recreate your tea experience at home.

You would have to travel to Somerset or the Cotswolds to find a more genuine Jane Austen eatery. Laura Ashley chintz and lace abound. The wood-panel wainscoted walls are brightened by gilded mirrors and an endless collection of brightly-colored tea wares lining the room. Floral curtains, wicker chairs and puffy pillows give the feel of an comfortable English cottage.

The décor is just the beginning of your state-side journey into British cuisine. The menu is filled with culinary classics lifted from the pages of an English tea room. Included in the offerings are favorites such as Shepherd's Pie, Curry Beef Pasties, crumpets, and scones with cream and strawberry jam.

The real jewel in the crown of this royal retreat is

a tea list that would be hard to find in a tea room in England. Over 50 teas fill the extensive inventory that boasts beautiful white, green, oolong and black teas, as well as herbal tisanes and flavored teas from around the world.

Why drink a common Earl Grey or English Breakfast when you can choose a Golden Puerh or a rare White Darjeeling? Each pot is made fresh and brought piping hot to the table in a press pot. With perfect flair, Queen Mary puts the "tea" in tea room!

Afternoon tea here can be as simple as a pot of tea with a Queen Mum Cookie, or a Royal Afternoon Tea featuring course after course of traditional savories and sweets complimented with a flute of sparkling wine. The crustless tea sandwiches, pastries and cakes are all made in-house by Mary and her talented staff. Many of the recipes have been handed down through the owner's family for generations. Luckily for regular customers, the menu changes regularly so that surprises await at each visit.

Queen Mary's royal theme often carries over to the customers fantasies. Is there a little princess in

your party? In the eyes of children, Queen Mary is a magical land where being a princess (or a prince) becomes reality. Whether it is birthday party for that special princess, or an end of school celebration, Queen Mary offers a Children's Afternoon Tea especially tailored for the tastes and appetites of young royals.

Adult ladies at tea also like to feel a bit regal sometimes. Don't be surprised to see a few diners wearing tiaras while dabbing clotted cream and preserves on their fresh scones.

"It's amazing how your day can change once you don a tiara," Mary likes to say.

The Queen-in-residence will lend you a faux-diamond diadem should you forgot to bring your own. It's just another of the countless details that she pays attention to daily. It's good to be the queen!

Touring suggestions: Like San Francisco, Seattle is a walking city with lots of great neighborhoods to visit and ethnic foods to discover.

The Pioneer Square area is home to Armandino Batali's Salumi, a tiny Italian meat and sandwich shop packed with flavorful cured meat, similar to what you might find in a Tuscan village. It is probably ten feet wide and thirty feet deep with a few tables and always a line of customers queued for carry-out. Armandino's famous son is New York chef and Food Network personality Mario Batali.

Tea lovers will not want to miss visiting The Teacup, a full service retail tea store and tea bar that has been in business on Queen Ann Avenue for more than 15 years. The historic Queen Ann Hill area is an energetic neighborhood bustling with family-owned businesses and ethnic eateries. Elizabeth Nottingham is the tea shop's owner and eager professor of tea knowledge.

No visit to Seattle is complete without a pilgrimage to the world famous Pike Street Market. Since its first day of business, August 17, 1907, when 10,000 visitors overwhelmed vendors, this has been Seattle's number one tourist draw. Sandwiched between the waterfront and the main drag of First Avenue, this extravagant exhibition of all things delicious is the hub of Seattle's vital culinary culture.

Today, the market easily draws up to 40,000 visitors on summer Saturday. It is a food lover's paradise packed with stall after stall of fresh vegetables, meats, baked goods, cheeses, herbs, and flowers displayed with an artistic flair that rivals the street markets of Paris and Florence.

Street performers, craftsmen, local artists, florists, fruit vendors, and the many specialty food shop employees are just a few of the folks vying for your attention as you wander through the 190 stalls and shops. With many choices available for informal sit down dining as well, you'll have a hard time deciding where to feast.

Be sure to watch out for flying fish. This is home of one of the best known fishmongers in America and they love to amuse, and torment, out-of-towners with their fish flinging flair.

ROSE TREE COTTAGE

Pasadena, California

The picture-perfect setting of Pasadena, California has long been home to one of America's great tea treasures. For nearly two decades, The Rose Tree Cottage and owners, Edmund and Mary Fry, have set the standard for serving a proper afternoon tea. This is the venerable English couple that ignited the tea revolution in Southern California.

"When you come to Rose Tree Cottage," says Edmund, "You come to experience a little piece of England and to be transported, if only temporarily, back to a romantic and nostalgic time." Rose Tree Cottage is actually a historical monument, one of five miniature English storybook thatched cottages built in the 1920s. The gardens, courtyard and buildings are covered with roses and are surrounded by emerald green lawns that face the San Gabriel Mountains. The tea room sits just minutes from the Rose Bowl and the fantastic Huntington Library and Gardens.

The interior is a scene lifted from a Yorkshire country home. One side table is covered with a who's who collection of celebrity photographs featuring the well-known guests, film stars, dignitaries and members of the Royal Family who have found refuge here over the years. The Frys received an accolade from a special guest when His Royal High-

ness, the Prince of Wales, visited and pronounced the Rose Tree Cottage a "sterling sight."

Tea is served in three rooms: a large sunny side room, a cozy window-filled sunroom and, everyone's favorite, a parlor with an enticing fireplace surrounded by a few small tables and comfortable upholstered chairs. The window table has an appealing view of English roses and California palms seen through lace curtains.

Guests are surrounded by shelf after shelf of British memorabilia and serenaded by the soft melodies of English music from a bygone era. The sound of clinking bone china cups and saucers mixes with the sweet fragrance of hot scones and fresh roses.

In a setting reminiscent of a Daphne DuMaurier novel, each guest is seated by the ever-attentive proprietor, dressed appropriately in black tails and white gloves. First time visitors soon realize he takes his role as host seriously while effortlessly directing the countless cues that go into this daily drama, but all are quickly put at ease by his affable demeanor and charm. Mr. Fry serves a never ending pot of his signature English Village Tea, a mellow Ceylon and Indian blend that is perfect for a relaxing experience.

The Frys and their busy staff serve a traditional Full Afternoon Tea featuring a selection of finger sandwiches (prawn, cucumber, and Tipperary

ish teapots and china. One room has the look of an English grocery, offering nearly 250 flavors of tea, British foods, cookbooks, and a refrigerated display case with scones, sausage rolls, and other baked goods ready to take home.

Edmund and Mary Fry have earned a well-deserved national reputation for offering a proper tea to thirsty Americans. Their passionate devotion to Edmund's British roots has given them a vocation where they share themselves liberally with all who come through the door of their cherished Rose Tree Cottage. Those who live in the vicinity are fortunate to have such a neighbor where they may refresh themselves regularly. It's as convenient as being in England - without the jet lag.

Touring suggestion: The Huntington Library, Art Collections and Botanical Gardens is one of the highlights of any trip to Pasadena. This is home to Gainesborough's Blue Boy and other British masterpieces. Stroll the 120 acres of breathtaking gardens and enjoy an informal tea in the Rose Garden Tea Room.

cheese), and freshly baked scones with lashings of Devon cream and their own delicious preserves. To complete the never-ending treat there is a selection of sweets, including the famous Rose Tree Cottage shortbread and Sticky Toffee Pudding. Every beautiful morsel is served on fine Royal Albert Bone China.

Miss Moppet is another hardworking family member. The 'Sole Cat Proprietor' of Rose Tree Cottage is the official greeter. When not napping, she takes her job very seriously. After the first Rose Tree Cottage cat was cat-napped, this regal feline appeared as a tiny calico kitten left in a gift bag with a note that said "We hope she'll make you happy again". That was years ago and Miss Moppet since has made thousands of friends. Her favorite food, of course, is Devonshire Cream from a tea patron's saucer.

The Frys offer everything imaginable for gifts and home accessories from England. This is one of the finest British shops in the Los Angeles area. The colorful cottage is filled to the brim with Brit-

SAMOVAR TEA LOUNGE

San Francisco, California

There is a whiff of the exotic when you enter the Samovar Tea Lounge. If your idea of a tea room is a pink cottage filled with frilly Victorian tables and chintz teapots, you are in for a surprise. This is not your grandmother's tea room! Considering the history of tea in this maritime city, it was only a matter of time before the idea of a pan-Asian tea room came to the mind of Jesse Jacobs, and Samovar Tea Lounge was born.

Strategically located on a street corner between the Mission and Castro districts, the original Samovar is a prime example of how tea is putting on a new face in America. You won't find ladies in hats drinking raspberry tea and eating crustless finger sandwiches here. What you will find is a mix of young professionals, college students and neighborhood regulars who drop by every day to enjoy a pot of tea and a bento box while catching up with the lives of their fellow tea friends. The convivial spirit of this tea sanctuary causes a pause in a busy day. Customers often linger for hours as the gentle morning sunshine streams through the wall of glass windows and onto their backs.

Most people know a samovar is an Eastern European boiler that heats water for tea. Drinking tea around a samovar with friends leads to a warm and comforting environment. Samovar Tea Lounge is founded on that tradition of relaxation and social intimacy. For modern San Franciscans, Samovar is a soothing alternative to noisy liquor bars where friends gather to socialize.

A working samovar sits at the center of the restaurant puffing steam across the teacup-laden bar. Intimate two-seat tables fill the room. A raised platform draws attention to the end of the sunshine-filled café where a long wooden table is placed so that eight to ten guests can sit on straw mats. A 400-year-old statue of Bodhisattva Kuan Yin presides over the gathering. For private parties, a gauzy curtain wraps around the guests like a temple veil.

The emphasis here is on tea. Where else can you find an offering of nine puerhs, each with the vintage year listed on the menu? Green, oolong and herbal teas are the most popular choices. Sure, black teas are listed but customers are more into orange ginger than Earl Grey. A myriad of Asian teapots and clay tea bowls stand stacked and ready to brew leaves in a variety of ways.

Such a stunning collection of teas can only be paired with equally fascinating foods. Samovar serves beautiful dishes, often involving tea in their preparation. Guests may munch on a small bowl of the green tea-dusted pumpkin seeds or a piece of Karter's Toffee as they sip a cup of Kukicha or Keemun Hao Ya.

One popular dish is Zuke, a tea soup. A pot of green tea is served along with a bowl filled with Napa cabbage, oolong rice and seaweed. Pour the tea into the bowl and your meal is served.

For a bit of Russian flavor, try the Odessa Platter. It includes smoked trout, caviar, red onion, chopped egg, and rye crackers. The menu also offers a selection of small plates, similar to tapas. These might include an artichoke tart, wild salmon tea toasts or lapsang tuna skewers.

And of course there's High Tea served in various fashions: English High Tea, Japanese High Tea, Russian High Tea or Moorish High Tea. Each comes with the sweets, savories, and traditions associated with the culture.

The growing appeal of this cultural and gastronomical oasis has, like all strong business models, spurred a clone. There's now a second location of Samovar Tea Lounge in the Yerba Buena Gardens. It's located on top of the Martin Luther King Jr. fountain in the Moscone Convention Center neighborhood. It sits like a jewel box above the fountains and although encased in glass, this location is as warm an environment as the original.

The mission of Samovar Tea Lounge is to bring cultures together into a new concept that captures the essence of international tea traditions in a contemporary way. The owners believe that as more people experience the tea lifestyle, the world will become a better place.

San Francisco, with its vast variety of tea shops and tea rooms from which to choose, has become the gateway to tea in America. At the Samovar Tea lounge, the 5000 year tradition of tea has never been fresher.

ST. JAMES TEAROOM

Albuquerque, New Mexico

A visit to Albuquerque allows you to experience the authentic Southwest. One of the oldest cities in the U.S., Albuquerque boasts a unique multicultural heritage and history where Native American, Hispanic & Latino, Anglo and other cultural influences are a part of everyday life. A meal at most local restaurants is accented by the smoke-kissed flavor of freshly roasted green chilies and the earthy fruitiness of red chile sauce, both essential to New Mexican dishes like burritos, stacked enchiladas and stuffed sopaipillas. Amidst all this spiciness, Albuquerque has to be one of the most unlikely settings for one of America's great tea rooms.

The St. James Tearoom is located on the west side of Rio Grande Boulevard near Old Town. It's off the street and tucked away inside a collection of offices and shops called The Rio Grande Plaza.

It took a tea lover like Mary Alice Higbie to conceive the idea of opening an English tea room in this unlikely part of the world. A tea drinker since an early age, Mary Alice prepared for her new venture by visiting British tea establishments and receiving certification through Dorothea Johnson's Tea and Etiquette program. She opened The St. James Tearoom with two employees on December 22, 1999 and her tea business took off immediately. Within six months of opening, this tea haven received a four stars rating by the Albuquerque Journal and the title of "Best New Restaurant" in Albuquerque by *La Cocinita* magazine.

It wasn't long before this tea entrepreneur realized she needed more hands, and her son Daniel volunteered to become her general manager. Freshly educated with a Master of Arts in International Relations and equipped with a bit of British flair leftover from his time as an exchange student at Oxford University, this savvy son adds a masculine influence not often seen in tea rooms.

Daniel hosts an annual Cigar Tea held each spring on the patio, of course. Men and women gather as the beautiful New Mexico sun sets to enjoy an evening complete with a three-course dinner tea, fine cigars, and a sampling of fortified wines such as Sherry, Port, and Madeira. Prince Albert would have felt right at home in this setting.

Special events are all a part of what keeps loyal customers coming back again and again. Other regular themed events hosted here include A Celtic Cel-

menu changes seasonally and includes traditional tea foods, such as cucumber or sprig of watercress served on thin bread with a bit of herbed butter, as well as imaginative new creations that keep customers coming back again and again to see what delights this fabulous kitchen might concoct next.

The sweets are often more than you can appreciate in one setting and carry-outs are frequently seen in the hands of happy guests making their way back into the bright southwestern sunshine. These delicious desserts include such temptations as Strawberry Mead Syllabub, Tipsy Tart with Irish Whiskey & Milk Chocolate Cream, or Pistachio Cookies.

The tea selections here are as complete as anyone might desire in a traditional tea room. One of the most requested is the Buckingham Palace Garden Party, a lightly scented Earl Grey blended by Her Majesty's tea blender. Be sure to ask Mary Alice to tell you the story behind her acquisition of that recipe.

No tea room is complete without a gift shop. The Cherriwyn China Shop is the perfect place to

ebration, An Evening with Jane Austen, Etiquette Teas for all ages, Father Daughter Teas, and Life Is Sweet Pink Teas for Breast Cancer Awareness.

The immediate charm of this hideaway is the unique way Mary Alice has laid out the dining areas in this limited space. Private alcoves, more like British parlors, are arranged with names like Magdalen, Aberystwyth, Bannockburn, St. Bees, Glamis, Gwynedd, Magdalen, Stow on Wold, and Tintagel. Most accommodate two to six people while one real room seats a dozen guests at table. Each is furnished with period stuffed chairs and sofas and accented with low tables, antique lamps and Victorian books and bric-a-brac. The relaxed atmosphere tends to encourage conversation. Servers in period dress complete this theatrical setting.

The set afternoon tea is served on an elegant three-tiered tray. This is a full meal which includes savories and tea sandwiches, two different types of scones or breads, including the St. James traditional Cream Scones, and a variety of sweets and desserts. All are handmade on site by the chef. The

find gifts as you enter or exit St. James. They carry a beautiful array of fine china, lace and linens for your table, hats, gloves, books about tea, note cards and many smaller gifts, and of course, a complete selection of fine quality loose teas.

One of the main missions of the St. James Tearoom is to give customers a full English tea experience. They have far surpassed that goal. It would be hard to find a tea shop in Great Britain offering an afternoon tea that is more satisfying and deliciously elegant.

Touring suggestions: New Mexico is one of those places you need to visit every now and then to clear your mind and reconnect with the great outdoors. "Outdoors" is in great abundance here.

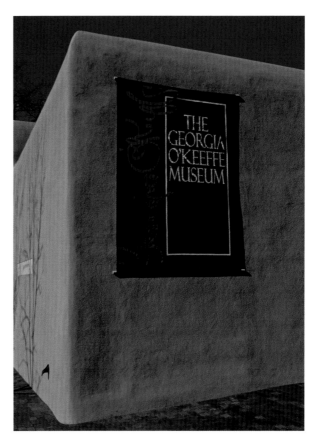

One way to take in the landscape is to drive to Bandelier National Monument. Best known for mesas, sheer-walled canyons, and the ancestral Pueblo dwellings found among them, Bandelier also includes over 23,000 acres of designated wilderness and miles of open sky.

Albuquerque is conveniently located an hour from Santa Fe and a wealth of southwestern art and world-class restaurants. One of the highlights is the Georgia O'Keefe Museum located in the center of town, steps from the Palace of The Governors. Be sure to make your way through the art galleries of Canyon Road and stop for an informal cup of tea at The Teahouse.

The High Road from Santa Fe to Taos leads to the most visited church in New Mexico, Santuario de Chimayó. Over 300,000 people visit this sacred site every year. Believed to be built on sacred earth with miraculous healing powers, the legendary shrine El Santuario de Chimayó houses the crucifix which began the original shrine, but for some reason its curative powers have been overshadowed by El Posito, the "sacred sand pit" from which it sprang.

The drive to Taos takes you along beautiful mountain roads to the town filled with art and gift shops. A working pueblo can be seen near the town before taking the road that circles back to Santa Fe and Albuquerque.

THE ST. REGIS HOTEL

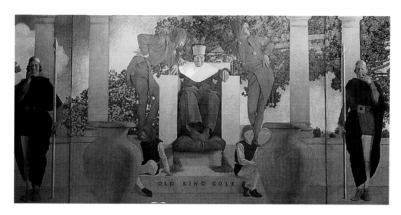

New York, New York

A slow spin through a golden revolving door encapsulated with Beaux Arts filigree is all it takes to leave the bustle of Fifth Avenue behind. You have entered a serene refuge of a time long past. A man wearing a tails and white gloves disappears around a marble column - the ghost of John Jacob Astor or a St. Regis doorman? Inside the wood paneled elevator, you hear the light tinkle of crystal from the Waterford chandelier. You wonder if you have somehow escaped the modern world.

For nearly a century, The St. Regis has remained a center of New York's civic, business and social life. The hotel was completely restored in 1988. To keep its golden image as one of the world's premier hotels, 2,500 sheets of 22k gold leaf were applied, making it the second largest gold leafing project ever undertaken in the United States. All that glittering gold is illuminated by 6,000 crystal chandeliers and reflected by over three acres of marble and 2,400 decorative mirrors. The opulent interior has the look of a Viennese palace rather than a hotel. Guests are made to feel like royalty with the services of an on-floor butler, on duty 24 hours and waiting to take care of any need.

Completed in 1904, the 18-story building designed by architects Trowbridge and Livingston was the tallest building in the area at the time and a source of wonderment to visitors. It was declared a New York City Landmark 84 years later.

The site of the hotel, at Fifth Avenue and 55th Street, was a residential neighborhood when Colonel John Jacob Astor IV broke ground for it in 1902. He spared no expense in creating a hotel of world class luxury and taste. The hotel cost $5.5 million to construct. It was lavishly furnished with antique tapestries, oriental rugs, and antique Louis XV furniture. A library of 3,000 leather-bound, gold-tooled classic and current books was provided for the hotel's guests and cared for by a private librarian. Colonel Astor was used to fine surroundings. After all, he had spent many summers at his parents' Beechwood mansion in Newport, Rhode Island.

Astor wanted to create a hotel where gentlemen and their families could feel as comfortable as they would as guests in a private home; in fact, he frequently used The St. Regis as a place for his personal guests and visiting relatives to stay at his invitation. For their comfort, he introduced such modern conveniences as telephones in very room, a fire alarm system, central heating and an air-cooling system that efficiently predated modern air conditioning and allowed each guest to control the temperature of his room. Mail chutes were installed on each floor, a newsworthy innovation at that time.

hung over the bar at Astor's Knickerbocker Hotel in New York.

Leading to the bar lies one of the world's most sophisticated rooms for enjoying tea. Raised on a balustraded dais, the Astor Court appears suspended under a pale, frothy sky, encircled by a mythological mural, painted by Zhou Shu Liang, depicting the Greek ideals of peace, harmony and beauty. In colors of white, gold and pink, it is as confectionery in spirit as the three-course tea offered each afternoon.

The Court's dozen or so tables cluster around a central statue banked by flowers. Table settings and exquisite linens from Porthault and porcelain from Limoges by way of Tiffany & Company, are exclusive to the hotel. Eighteen choices of tea are presented in silver teapots to the soothing music of a harp. Rock candy sugar sticks, both amber and crystalline, to dip into your tea at whim, add a sweet touch. Champagne, sherries and desert wines also are offered for an additional price.

One of the hotel's other novel features was a special design "for the disposition of dust and refuse," one of the first central vacuum systems. All maids had to do was plug their vacuum cleaner hoses into sockets situated throughout the hotel.

The St. Regis soon became the center of Manhattan social life and headquarters for the original "400" list, the elite social group chosen by Colonel Astor's mother. This coveted roster of socially acceptable folk was influenced or even drawn up by her.

Colonel Astor died when the Titanic sank in 1912, leaving the St. Regis to his son, Vincent Astor. Feeling he was too immersed in other real estate ventures to devote the necessary time, he quickly sold the hotel to Duke Management (the tobacco Duke family) who in 1927 expanded the hotel to 540 rooms by extending it along East 55th Street.

The hotel's most famous decoration, the King Cole mural, was installed behind the bar in 1932. The puckish mural by Maxfield Parrish had been given to Colonel Astor by the artist and earlier

The gilt and grandeur of this opulent tea room may appear intimidating at first glance. But New York is a cramped and crowded place. With its high ceilings, comfortable armchairs, soft light and gorgeous flowers, afternoon tea in the Astor Court is the cure for regaining your sanity. Somewhere, cars are honking and cell phones are ringing, but, at least for now, that world can wait. You are having tea with the ghost of Colonel Astor.

Touring suggestions: The St. Regis sits at the heart of one of New York's most opulent retail districts. Both Tiffany & Company and Bergdorf Goodman are Fifth Avenue neighbors. The Japanese department store Takashimaya is adjacent to the St. Regis. Takashimaya's Tea Box Restaurant is a Fifth Avenue secret treasure. This lower level private space accommodates 60 people for lunch or tea. Japanese Chef Taro Mitsuiki can craft a menu to remember, including unique Bento Box presentations. The beautiful display of loose leaf teas is a sensory delight.

If all this decadent consumerism becomes overwhelming, you might want to step across Fifth Avenue for evensong at St. Thomas Church. The church is home to one of the premier choirs in New York City. Also, St. Patrick's Cathedral, with its soaring spires, is just a few blocks away.

If it's art that feeds your soul, the new Museum of Modern Art (MOMA) is located just off Fifth Avenue on West 53rd Street. The building itself is a work of art not to be missed. The Terrace V Cafe on the fifth floor is a perfect place to enjoy a pot of tea at the conclusion of your museum tour.

The newly refurbished Plaza Hotel at the corner of Fifth Avenue and Central Park is home to one of the most expensive afternoon teas in New York City. The famous Palm Court has long been a favorite gathering spot for well-to-do visitors from all over the world.

End your afternoon with a stroll through Central Park. It's a great way to walk off a few of the tea time calories you enjoyed while drinking in this tea-infused city.

TEA LEAVES & THYME

Woodstock, Georgia

Tea room owners often call on family and friends to help them realize their dream. This is certainly true for Georgia's Kim Jordy. Kim called on the resources of her parents, sons, spouse and a best friend to help make her Tea Leaves and Thyme tea room one of the most popular destinations for tea in the Atlanta area.

Kim traces her love of tea to her mother who, being of British descent, always had a cup of tea in her hand. She infused tea into Kim's life from an early age and sparked a passion for tea that continues to this day.

Her father was a classically trained chef and restaurateur. When Kim decided to open her tea room a decade ago, he was there to advise and encourage her. Best of all, he made the tables for her new tea room.

The three Jordy sons, now young men, each contributed to the success of their mother's adventure when they were younger. Today, they help when needed on weekends. Caleb and Zachery both spend time in the "back of the house" preparing food and washing dishes while Jason utilizes his mechanical skills repairing appliances and anything else that might need attention in this busy workplace.

Kim's husband Glynn can often be found hosting on weekends as he seats guests and lends a masculine touch to the mainly feminine retreat where women and young girls love to celebrate every special occasion in their lives. The Jordys have watched a number of young ladies grow up through a progression of birthday parties, bridal teas and baby showers enjoyed at Tea Leaves and Thyme. Tea has been the center of countless celebrations in this area.

The town of Woodstock, now a bedroom community of Atlanta, was once a railroad town where thousands of bales of cotton were loaded on trains bound for mills across the country. The restored depot still sits beside the L&N railway tracks in the center of town but the long freight trains now rumble through without stopping.

Kim's longtime friend Suzanna Spollen helped cultivate her desire to open a tea business at a time when the concept of hot tea in the land of sweet tea was just beginning to catch on. The two tea partners sat around a kitchen table for a year tasting teas and looking through merchandise catalogs developing the concept of what a Georgia tea room should be. They knew that they would have to make it a fun gathering place for women of all ages. They stocked one room with party dresses, boas and fun hats so that guests could act out their dream characters while drinking tea. It's amazing how uninhibited a guest can feel while wearing a hat and boa! Suzanna continues to manage the re-

drink peach and flavored teas are becoming more and more "tea savvy." They now ask for single estate Darjeelings, Japanese green tea or Chinese white tea. Kim continues studying to keep up with their maturing tastes and tea trends that are influencing today's educated tea consumer.

Along with a full lunch menu, Kim offers tea service throughout the day. The choices include a Full Afternoon Tea with seasonal fresh fruit, freshly baked scones with lemon curd and Amaretto cream, assorted tea sandwiches, miniature tea desserts, and a choice of chicken salad or a sun-dried tomato tartlet. A lighter version is also available. For a quick retreat, a traditional British cream tea is offered. Children are not overlooked here. A Mad Hatter's Children's Tea is served with fruit tea, scones, a peanut butter and jelly heart-shaped sandwich dipped in chocolate, a raspberry rabbit tea sandwich with a marshmallow tail, a ham striped tea sandwich, a chocolate chip cookie and a chocolate cherry mouse.

Kim's contribution to the vitality of Woodstock is evident by the number of travelers who make the

tail shop that is filled with everything needed for an at home tea experience.

Kim opened her first location with seating for 25. It became so popular that she soon increased the capacity to 40. That soon proved too small for tea lovers who came from across the Atlanta area and surrounding states. After five years, Kim relocated to a century-old house in the heart of town. The tea room, like a southern home, has a warm and hospitable feel. The four dining rooms are named for women who lived in the home. A picture of each hangs over the fireplace. There is the Georgia Carpenter Dawson Room (named after the original owner), the Sarah Dawson Parr Room, the Francis Hawthorne Green Room, and the Elizabeth Waldrop Peerdon Room. The bright and cheerful front porch is named "Mary's Porch" in honor of Mary Hughes.

The tea list at Tea Leaves and Thyme is complete with seventy selections and it continues to grow. Customers who were drawn here a decade ago to

journey here to enjoy tea and then wander through the local shops and city park. She is feeding a growing tea culture that is becoming more and more aware of the civilizing and calming effects of tea. Although some may have come for the chance to dress up and make-believe, many are now getting serious about tea. And the exciting addition that Kim sees on a daily basis is more and more of her guests are men. Way to go, Glynn!

Touring suggestions: Woodstock is just north of Atlanta and the outlying towns of Marietta and Roswell. Its location makes it easily accessible not only from Atlanta, but also from Birmingham, Chattanooga and Asheville.

Atlanta has a host of attractions to keep visitors of all ages happy. Two easy downtown activities include tours of CNN or the World of Coca-Cola. Also at hand is the world's largest aquarium. The Georgia Aquarium is home to more than 100,000 animals of 500 different species and eight million gallons of fresh and marine water with five galleries depicting different habitats.

Downtown Atlanta is home to Martin Luther King's neighborhood. Explore his birth home, historic Ebenezer Baptist Church and The King Center. The grave site of Dr. King and his wife, Coretta Scott King, are also located at The King Center. The Jimmy Carter Presidential Library is just a few minutes away from the King Center, or drive through the Virginia Highlands, best known for its restaurants, pubs, galleries and streets lined with vintage homes.

Peachtree Street leads to Midtown Atlanta. This neighborhood is coming alive with new restaurants, boutique hotels and shops. At the center of this area's renaissance is The Woodruff Center, home of the Atlanta Symphony and The High Museum of Art. The High is home to the finest collection of art found in the southeastern United States. A short stroll toward downtown leads to the Margaret Mitchell house and the Fox Theatre. Both are must-sees for fans of the book and movie, "Gone With the Wind."

THE TEA ROOM

Savannah, Georgia

If ever there was an American city that was a perfect location for the enjoyment of afternoon tea, it is the beautiful coastal city of Savannah, Georgia. Hospitality, landscape and architecture all come together in this historic setting to serve as the backdrop for one of the South's finest tea presentations.

The inspiration for The Tea Room of Savannah was sparked a century ago in far-off Glasgow, Scotland. Mary Cranston, a prominent Victorian tea room entrepreneur, commissioned art nouveau artist and architect, Rennie Mackintosh, to design five tea rooms in the city. They were bold and organic in style. So complete was his vision that he created not only the building, but also the furniture, leaded glass windows, murals, and light fixtures. Even his unique calligraphy was used on the menus and signage. His avant garde creations are well-known today by students of both tea and architecture. Thousands of Mackintosh devotees make the pilgrimage to Glasgow to see his last remaining tea room still in operation, The Willow Tea Room on Sauchiehall Street.

Savannah's Elizabeth Ruby became a fan of Mackintosh long before she ever dreamed of opening a tea room. Her love of his modernistic designs compelled her to recreate his vision in Georgia.

Mackintosh and Miss Cranston would be proud to know that The Tea Room of Savannah is one of several restored Broughton Street businesses that are once again bringing new life, and loyal customers, to this once-bustling retail district of one of America's most sophisticated southern cities.

From the time you walk through the door of The Tea Room, you know you are in a serious tea shop. As is the case at Mariage Frères in Paris or Bettys of York, row after row of tea canisters are the first things you see lining the shelves behind the front counter. Elizabeth is a serious student of tea. She sat at the feet of many tea experts over the years as she honed her craft. She spends much time discovering new teas and sourcing teas her customers request. Over 50 selections of fine quality teas from around the world await your choosing. Each is expertly brewed for the customer according to correct water temperature and steeping time. And if you find something you wish to experience again, you may buy a few ounces to take home for your next tea party.

Like many who fall victim to the mesmerizing influence of Mackintosh, Elizabeth was inspired to follow her dream of creating a tea room with as many of the artist's touches as she could employ and afford. High-back chairs, low light lamps, an-

squares. The city is proud to be home to one of the largest National Landmark Historic Districts in the United States. This 2.5-mile area, which runs from River Street to Forsyth Park, formed a vital part of General James Edward Oglethorpe's original city plan when he founded Savannah in 1733. This area is filled with quaint shops, historic churches, charming boutiques and world-class restaurants nestled beneath a canopy of moss-covered live oak trees.

Savannah is a city best explored by walking. Search out familiar movie settings from "Midnight in the Garden of Good and Evil" or Forest Gump's park bench. At dusk, walk hand-in-hand with your partner along the riverfront and wave at ships moving freight upriver. This perfect blending of architectural and nature could be the reason General William Tecumseh Sherman could not bring himself to burn this magnificent city on his relentless march to the sea in 1863. Instead, he presented it as a Christmas gift to his commander-in-chief, President Lincoln, and one of America's great gems was saved. Thank goodness he did.

tiques, and potted plants all add to the comfortable feeling of this soothing sanctuary. Much of the eclectic mix of china and linens was gathered from the wealth of antique shops in this area.

This is an atmosphere conducive to conversation and lingering afternoons. An inviting fireplace adds a relaxing air to the library dining room where tea and books could easily convince a guest to spend a few hours. As was the case in Miss Cranston's Scottish tea rooms, the customer here is offered a tempting variety of scones, pastries, soups, sandwiches, and cakes. Each is made fresh daily in Elizabeth's kitchen. The tea services include Cream Tea, Light Tea, Soup Tea, Salad Tea, Lunch Tea, Children's Tea, Afternoon Tea, Full Afternoon Tea or Royal Afternoon Tea. This is Georgia and the summers along the coast can be quite hot and humid. Iced tea is offered to take the heat off the most oppressive summer days. Don't confuse it with the "sweet tea" found in most area restaurants. This is real tea steeped with whole tea leaves.

After tea, you may want to take a leisurely stroll through Savannah's historic 22 azalea-filled

Touring suggestions: America's largest commercial tea growing operation, Bigelow's Charleston Tea Plantation, lies 2 1/2 hours north of Savannah, Georgia and 45 minutes south of Charleston, South Carolina.

The history of American grown tea has its unique roots in the soil of the coastal lowlands. The Federal Department of Agriculture began a tea research farm in Summerville, north of Charleston, in 1884. It closed after four years because the government concluded the climate was too unstable to produce a profitable crop.

In 1888, Dr. Charles Shepard planted 100 acres of tea plants on his Summerville Pinehurst Farm. One of the problems of making American tea profitable was the cost of labor. The government estimated the "minimum cost about eight times as much to pick one pound of tea in South Carolina as that paid for the same service in Asia." In addition, the optimal climate for growing tea wasn't healthy for field workers.

Dr. Shepard addressed the problem of securing laborers for the fields by opening a school and making tea-picking part of its curriculum, essentially ensuring a force of child labor while providing them with an education they might not otherwise obtain. His optimistic spirit looked promising when he won the tea-drinking public's esteem at the 1904 St. Louis World's Fair where his oolong tea took first prize. His death in 1915 ended the Summerville experiment and the plants were abandoned. Interestingly enough, the original farm is now a subdivision and, in the older sections of Summerville, tea bushes serve as yard hedging.

In 1960, the Lipton Company rescued many of the original tea plants to open a research facility on Wadmalaw Island. Again, this venture was not profitable. It was in 1987 that Bill Hall, a third-generation tea taster and tea maker, realized his passion in life and, with a business partner, acquired ownership of the Charleston Tea Plantation. American Classic Tea was born.

In 2003, Bigelow Tea purchased the plantation. Mr. Hall and the Bigelow family have partnered together in a mission to build Charleston Tea Plantation into a beautiful, informative and educational tourist destination. Today they have successfully built Charleston Tea Plantation into a "must see" adventure for tea lovers and tourists alike who visit the area from around the world.

WINDSOR COURT HOTEL

New Orleans, Louisiana

In a city steeped in French and Spanish tradition, the Windsor Court Hotel offers a touch of England in the heart of New Orleans. Designed to replicate the interior of a stately English manor, the hotel features antiques and period reproductions from the 17th and 18th century. Decorated in soft, restful colors, the lobby and public rooms are tastefully crafted with high ceilings, intricate moldings, rich woods, beautiful marble and woven floor coverings that add to the civilized sense of tradition.

After opening in February 1984 with Princess Anne presiding over the festivities, the hotel caught the eye of anglophile James Sherwood, chairman of Orient-Express Hotels. In 1991 the award-winning retreat joined his collection of renowned hotels, trains, cruises and safaris.

Providing focal points in every room are original art works. Many of the pieces are of British origin with an emphasis on works that depict the hotel's namesake, Windsor Castle, and life of British royalty. The collection has an estimated value of more than $8 million and includes original works by Reynolds, Gainsborough and Huysman.

One of New Orleans's most beloved traditions is the Windsor Court's grand Afternoon Tea, cosseted English-style in the gracious surroundings of Le Salon. This comfortable retreat, just off the lobby, has hosted thousands of guests and several celebrities over the years. When rocker Rod Stewart stays at the hotel he enjoys afternoon tea with his own porcelain teapot that is stored at the hotel, ready for his return visits. Other celebrity fans have included Steve Martin, Eric Clapton, Paul McCartney, Kathy Lee Gifford, Ellen Degeneres, The Duchess of York, Nicholas Cage and Lisa Marie Presley.

You don't have to be a celebrity to receive star service here. Le Salon offers a full range of 20 loose-leaf teas steeped in delicate Wedgwood china. In the background, a harpist or a string trio performs. A pot of tea and beautiful music are just a prelude to the steady stream of beautiful tea foods that soon appear. The hotel's chefs produce more than 92,000 tea sandwiches annually for this fashionable pastime.

Delicious tea sandwiches they are with selections such as smoked turkey with a curry mayonnaise, poached salmon salad, egg salad with mango chutney, or cucumber with a dill sundried tomato cream cheese spread. The Royal Tea comes with the addition of smoked salmon canapés, caviar canapés and glass of sparkling wine, chardonnay or Spanish sherry. That's just the first course!

is consistently listed as one of the top hotels in the world.

Ladies should be aware that "withdrawing to the powder room" has turned into an oasis for guests of the Windsor Court Hotel. The ladies' room on the second floor features antique tables complete with makeup puffs, tissues, hand lotion and imported soaps, flower-laden cloth towels, and fresh flowers. Original artwork adorns elegantly upholstered walls while a Waterford crystal chandelier provides the most flattering lighting.

Whether visitors are drawn by food, jazz, history, architecture, the sultry sensuality or the laissez faire way of New Orleans, patrons of the afternoon tea at Windsor Court often leave with lasting memories of indulgence and pampering. After all, isn't that what a great American tea room experience is all about?

Touring suggestions: The hotel's location in the heart of the business district provides easy access to the French Quarter, the jazz clubs and restaurants of Bourbon Street, and the antique shops and art

The second course consists of scones with jams, lemon curd and Devonshire cream. The third course is a symphony of sweets, including chocolate dipped strawberries, chocolate truffles, tartlets, petits fours, and their signature strawberry cream swans. All the while, your pot of hot tea continues to be filled and the heavenly music never ends.

Just to make things more interesting, Le Salon features a monthly International Tea with a special savory and sweet item that celebrates the food of that country. For instance, April might feature Pai Mu Tan. This white tea from the Fujian province of China brews to a pale golden cup with a sweet, mellow taste. Food pairings for the month are two dim sum specialties. They include Seafood Sou which consists of shrimp, crabmeat, onions, peppers, celery, oyster sauce, and sesame oil wrapped in a puff pastry and a water chestnut cake. This attention to creative details is only one more reason why The Windsor Court

galleries of Royal Street. Hotel views to the south capture the Mississippi River, while the emerging Arts District is just blocks west.

A full day of touring should start, not with a sugary beignet and café au lait beside hundreds of tourists, but, with a hearty home-cooked meal at one of New Orlean's landmarks, Mother's Restaurant on nearby Poydras Street. After dining on grits and homemade biscuits, hop on an antique trolley for an easy ride through the Garden District and its wealth of antebellum architectural jewels.

Of course you can always escape the heat of the Louisiana gulf with a tour of the nearby Aquarium of the Americas, National D-Day Museum, or The Ogden Museum of Southern Art. For a memorable nightime excursion, the docks for the legendary paddle wheeler tours are all within a 15-minute walk.

While in the French Quarter, be sure to visit the city's centerpiece, St. Louis Cathedral. It's the only church where you can sit in a pew, meditate and listen to the far off strains of a Dixieland band all at the same time. It's an experience unique only to New Orleans.

Also unique to the area is the Acme Oyster Bar, the gathering place for raw oyster enthusiasts from around the world. The decor is simple and the prices are affordable. It's entertaining to watch the oyster shuckers prepare your plate in front of your eyes. Wash your oysters down with the local brew, Abita Beer or Abita Root Beer.

For tea lovers, one of the south's oldest tea rooms, The Bottom of the Cup, is just a couple of blocks off Bourbon Street. In a city that is home to the headquarters of Luzianne Iced Tea, how do they get customers to drink hot tea? By telling their fortunes. (You can't do that with iced tea!)

Established in 1929 when it was illegal to charge for fortune telling, The Bottom of the Cup set up shop on Chartres Street to sell cups of tea and "give away" tea leaf readings. Seventy five years later, the same family employs six psychics to keep up with the demand for tea and tea leaf readings. You can even have your tea leaves read over the phone. How do they do that?

GREAT TEA SHOPS of AMERICA

THE CULTURED CUP
Dallas, Texas

Dallas is home to one of the largest American retailers of France's famed Mariage Frères Tea. The Cultured Cup provides over 100 varieties of these world-renowned teas as well as a broad selection of teacups, teapots and accessories from around the globe. Proprietors Phil Krampetz and Kyle Stewart strive to ensure that this unique establishment, reminiscent of a European emporium, features an array of preparation and serving essentials not typically available in gourmet stores. This sophisticated gathering place also stocks imported drinking chocolates and 40 varieties of gourmet coffee.

8312 Preston Center Plaza Drive
Dallas, TX 75225
888.VIP.TEAS
www.culturedcup.com

THE PERENNIAL TEA ROOM
Seattle, Washington

THE TEA CUP
Seattle, Washington

Since 1990, the Perennial Tea Room has offered a vast array of tea and tea accessories to local tea drinkers and tourists from around the world. Located in the shadow of Historic Pike Place Market and around the corner from the original Starbucks, owners Sue Zuege and Julee Rosanoff love to dispense samples and information about their ever-growing family of teas. They host regular tea tastings, book signings, author dinners and classes catering to the local demand for more and more tea events. The expansive shop offers teapots for every possible brewing need.

1910 Post Alley
Seattle, WA 98101
888.448.4054
www.perennialtearoom.com

The Tea Cup has been dispensing quality specialty tea to thirsty customers in Seattle's historic Queen Anne Hill neighborhood for over 15 years. Proprietor Elizabeth Nottingham is passionate about tea and she loves to tell you about the vast array of world-class loose teas that line her walls while you sample a cup of First Flush Darjeeling or a rare pu-ehr. Her cozy shop is filled with shelf after shelf of teapots, cups and every tea accessory you could possibly need. In a city known for coffee, The Tea Cup is slowly converting new tea drinkers one cup at a time.

2207 Queen Anne Avenue. N
Seattle, WA 98109
877.841.4890
www.seattleteacup.com

TEA EMBASSY
Austin, Texas

Carol and Bob Sims, with son Jonathan, serve as tea's ambassadors to the fortunate residents of the sophisticated university city of Austin. More than a tea store, this is a learning center where regular seminars and tastings are held to introduce and enlighten eager students of tea to the 100 or so world-class loose teas stocked on the Sims' shelves. The downtown business is located in the historic Campbell-Miller house, built in 1872. This home-like environment, coupled with the hosts' Southern charm, makes this a perfect place to sample teas, purchase tea steeping equipment, and pick up a bit of tea knowledge. Be sure to check out their tea cookbook, *Tea Treasures*.

900 Rio Grande Street
Austin, Texas 78701
512.330.9991
www.teaembassy.com

TEANCE
Berkeley, California

Tea is hotter than ever in Berkeley, thanks in large part to young entrepreneurs like Winnie Yu, owner of Teance. After moving to the United States from Hong Kong, she found it difficult to find quality unblended teas. She decided to import the teas herself. She shares her tea finds and dispenses tea brewing advice at her tea bar and store located in one of Berkeley's most popular retail areas. She commands this tea wonderland from the center of a sleek concrete and copper gaiwan-shaped tea bar where she steeps and pours winter-picked wulong, Formosa Baochong and other rare treasures. With temptations like this, few customers leave empty-handed.

1780 4th Street
Berkeley, CA 94710
510.524.2832
www.teance.com

TEAISM
Washington, District of Columbia

TEA SOURCE
St. Paul, Minnesota

Michelle Brown and Linda Orr opened the first Teaism in 1996 in busy Dupont Circle. They took their name from the classic *Book of Tea* by Okakura Kakuzo. As eager students of tea, they began a zealous mission to share tea's richness and complexity. They immediately drew a thirsty crowd from the nearby universities, offices and embassies. One tea house became two tea houses, and soon there was a third within sight of the White House. Their empire of three Asian-influenced tea rooms and shops is a major source for quality loose tea and tea knowledge. Plus, their ginger scones are world-famous after being discovered by the Food Network.

For over a dozen years, the Midwest's pre-eminent authority on specialty tea has been Bill Waddington, owner of TeaSource. Bill travels the world in search of rare and exceptional teas. He is a frequent speaker at international tea events and can be heard regularly with Lynne Rosetto-Kasper on the National Public Radio show, *The Splendid Table*. TeaSource has locations both in St. Paul and St. Anthony. Each shop has a wall of tea cannisters that keeps customers coming back again and again to see what new finds Bill has brought back from his latest excursion. The shops also carry an extensive line of tea accessories and tea books.

2009 R Street NW
Washington, DC 20009
877.8TEAISM
www.teaism.com

752 Cleveland Avenue South
St. Paul, MN 55116
877.768.7233
www.teasource.com

The English Rose, Pleasanton, California

Recipes

Ahrens Tea Cake

½ cup butter
1 cup sugar
2 eggs
2 teaspoons vanilla
2 cups all-purpose flour
2 teaspoons baking powder
1 teaspoon baking soda
1 cup sour cream

Preheat oven to 350° F.

Cream butter and sugar together and add eggs and vanilla. Combine and mix flour, baking powder and baking soda. Add to butter mixture. Fold in sour cream. Spoon half of the batter into a greased and floured bundt pan.

Filling

½ cup sliced almonds, toasted
2 teaspoons cinnamon
½ cup brown sugar

Combine almonds, cinnamon and brown sugar. Sprinkle onto the middle of the batter. Cover the filling with the remaining batter and bake for 35 minutes.

"Wouldn't it be dreadful to live in a country where they didn't drink tea?"

— Noel Coward

Amelia's Banana Cake

4 tablespoons unsalted butter (½ stick)
1½ cups sugar
2 large eggs
1 cup lightly mashed ripe bananas
1¼ cups unbleached flour
1 cup whole wheat flour
¾ teaspoon baking soda
½ teaspoon salt
½ teaspoon baking powder
¼ cup buttermilk
1 teaspoon vanilla

Preheat oven to 350° F. Cream butter and sugar until light. Add eggs, one at a time, and beat until combined well. Add bananas and continue to beat just until combined.

In another bowl, sift flours, salt, baking soda, and baking powder. Add to butter mixture, stirring until just combined. Add buttermilk and vanilla and stir until combined well.

Divide batter between two well-buttered, floured 9" cake pans. Bake for 25 to 30 minutes or until a cake tester inserted in center comes out clean. Let layers cool in pans on racks for 10 minutes, then invert onto racks and let cool completely.

Frosting

3 cups confectioners' sugar
6 tablespoons unsalted butter, softened
½ teaspoon salt
½ cup mashed banana
1 teaspoon lemon juice
½ teaspoon vanilla
1 to 2 bananas, sliced thick
toasted walnut halves for garnish

Combine sugar, butter, and salt. Beat until smooth. In another bowl, combine banana, lemon juice, and vanilla. Add banana mixture to sugar mixture and combine well, adding more sugar as needed.

Place 1 cake layer on a serving plate, frost with banana butter cream and top with banana slices. Place second layer on top of frosting and frost top with remaining butter cream. Garnish with toasted walnut halves.

Apricot Bars

⅔ cup dried apricots
1 stick unsalted butter, softened
¼ cup granulated sugar
1⅓ cups all-purpose flour
1 cup packed light brown sugar
2 large eggs
½ cup chopped walnuts
½ teaspoon baking powder
1 teaspoon vanilla
½ teaspoon salt
confectioners' sugar for dusting

Preheat oven to 350° F.

In a small saucepan, simmer apricots in water, covered, for 15 minutes. Drain, then cool to room temperature. Chop finely. Beat together butter, granulated sugar, and 1 cup flour with an electric mixer on medium speed, until mixture resembles coarse crumbs. Press evenly over bottom of a greased 8" square metal baking pan (do not use non-stick) and bake in the middle of oven until golden, about 25 minutes.

Beat together chopped apricots, brown sugar, eggs, walnuts, baking powder, vanilla, salt and remaining ⅓ cup flour on medium speed until combined well. Pour topping over crust and bake in middle of oven until topping is set and golden, 25 to 30 minutes more.

Cool in pan on a rack and cut into 12 bars. Dust with confectioners' sugar.

Baby Cakes

⅔ cup butter, room temperature
1¾ cups sugar
2 eggs
2 teaspoons vanilla extract
3 cups cake flour
2 teaspoons baking powder
¾ teaspoon salt
1¼ cups milk
whipped cream, slightly sweetened
fresh fruit, such as berries or kiwi

Preheat oven to 325° F.

Wash and dry 14 tin cans, 14 to 16 ounces each, or 14 small (1-cup) soufflé dishes; grease and flour insides. In large bowl of electric mixer, beat butter, sugar, eggs, and vanilla until fluffy. Beat 5 minutes on high speed, scraping bowl occasionally.

Combine flour, baking powder, and salt. Add dry ingredients to batter alternately with milk.

Spoon about ⅓ cup of batter into each prepared tin can. Bake until a toothpick inserted in center comes out clean, 25 to 30 minutes. (The tops will not brown.)

Remove to a wire rack and cool completely, until edges become dry and crusty. Run a knife around the inside of cans or dishes to loosen edges, tap on a counter, then turn cakes out; they should slide out easily.

With a serrated knife, cut off and discard the rounded tops of cakes. Turn cakes upside down so cut edges are on the bottom. Cut cakes into two layers and fill with whipped cream and fresh fruit.

For a fun presentation, use pinking shears to cut squares of colorful wrapping paper large enough to cover the center of your dessert plates. Serve the Baby Cakes on the wrapping-paper squares.

Banana Fritters

4 ripe bananas, mashed
¾ cup all-purpose flour
2 eggs, beaten
3 tablespoons sugar
vegetable oil
cinnamon sugar

In a bowl, combine first 4 ingredients. Mix thoroughly and beat slightly.

Grease a griddle with vegetable oil. Drop 1 full tablespoon of batter onto hot, greased griddle. Fry on both sides. Serve with cinnamon sugar.

Beatrice Sugar Cookies

½ cup butter, softened
1 cup powdered sugar
1 teaspoon vanilla
2 egg yolks
1⅓ cups all-purpose flour
½ cup blanched almonds
Powdered sugar for dusting

Cream butter and sugar together in mixer; add vanilla and egg yolks. Mix in flour and blanched almonds. Form into a ball. Refrigerate dough for 20 minutes.

Preheat oven to 350° F. Roll dough on a floured surface to desired thickness. Cut dough with a heart-shaped cookie cutter and place on ungreased cookie sheet. Bake for 12-15 minutes. Allow cookies to cool on baking sheet for only 5 minutes and then remove to a cooling rack. Dust with powdered sugar before serving. Makes 3 dozen cookies.

Bergamot Bread Pudding

1 lemon or Seville sour orange
2 cups milk
5 tablespoons loose leaf Earl Grey tea
5 cups bread cubes
½ cup golden raisins
1 cup raw sugar
1 tablespoon nutmeg
3 eggs
chopped walnuts
honey

Preheat oven to 375° F. Using a grater, remove zest from fruit.

In a sauce pan, slowly heat milk to below boil. Add tea to milk and steep for 5 minutes. Strain tea leaves from milk.

Place bread cubes and golden raisins in a large mixing bowl. Add tea-milk and mix lightly with a wooden spoon. Add zest, sugar, and nutmeg. Mix gently and set aside.

Beat eggs in a small bowl. Add eggs to the bread mixture and mix together thoroughly.

Coat a bundt pan with butter. Pour in mixture. Place bundt pan in hot-water bath in oven. Bake 40-50 minutes.

Spoon warm into serving bowls and top with walnuts and drizzled honey.

Candied Ginger Scones

3 cups all-purpose flour
5 tablespoons sugar
⅔ pound cold butter, unsalted
½ cup Australian Candied Ginger
5 eggs, large
1¼ cups 2% milk

Preheat oven to 350° F.

Mix dry ingredients and finely chopped candied ginger together. Cut in butter using a pastry cutter until it forms pea-size balls. Combine eggs and milk and incorporate into flour mixture. Let rest.

Roll out and cut to desired shape. Brush with egg wash or milk and then sprinkle with white sugar. Bake 20 minutes or until golden brown.

Serve scones with whipped Devonshire cream and fresh fruit preserves.

Carrot Cake

2 medium eggs
1 cup sugar
¾ cup oil
½ cup walnuts, finely chopped
1 cup all-purpose flour, sifted
8 ounces carrots, grated
1 teaspoon cinnamon
1 teaspoon baking soda

Preheat oven to 350° F. Grease and line a 7" round cake pan.

Beat eggs and sugar together until thick and very pale. Beat in oil gradually, and then fold in the rest of the cake ingredients using a metal spoon. Pour into prepared pan and bake for 45-50 minutes or until firm and a skewer comes out clean when inserted in the center.

Remove from oven and allow to cool in pan for 15 minutes before turning out on wire rack.

Topping

1½ cups confectioners' sugar
2 ounces butter, room temperature
3 ounces cream cheese
½ teaspoon vanilla

Beat all ingredients together until very smooth and fluffy. Spread over top of cake.

Chicken Bombay Sandwiches

2 cups chicken breast, cooked and slivered
½ cup bacon, cooked and minced
¾ cup white cheddar cheese, grated
¼ cup red bell pepper, chopped
2 tablespoons green onions, minced
salt and pepper to taste
1½ tablespoons curry powder
½ teaspoon ground turmeric
dash Tabasco
1 teaspoon garlic, chopped
1½ cups mayonnaise
1 package pita bread

In a large bowl, combine chicken, bacon, cheese, red pepper, and onion. Toss together. Add salt, pepper, curry powder, turmeric, Tabasco, and garlic. Add mayonnaise until desired consistency is achieved.

Toast pita bread. Place chicken spread on pita triangles. Garnish with grapes.

Chocolate Trifle Lorraine

4 ounces unsweetened baking chocolate, broken into pieces
4 tablespoons unsalted butter, softened
1⅔ cups boiling water
2⅓ cups unbleached all-purpose flour
2 cups sugar
½ cup sour cream
2 large eggs
2 teaspoons baking soda
1 teaspoon salt
1 teaspoon vanilla

Preheat oven to 350° F.

Butter and flour a 13" x 9" x 2" cake pan.

Combine chocolate, butter, and boiling water. Stir until smooth. With an electric mixer on low speed, add remaining ingredients until just combined. Do not over beat.

Pour batter into prepared cake pan and bake for 40 to 50 minutes or until a cake tester inserted in the center comes out clean. Let cake cool in the pan on a rack for 10 minutes.

Invert cake onto cooling rack and let cool completely.

Cut cake into cubes and let dry at room temperature for a few hours.

Chocolate Fudge

4 tablespoons unsalted butter (½ stick)
1½ cups chocolate chips
¾ cup heavy cream
2½ cups confectioners' sugar, sifted
1 teaspoon vanilla

Combine all ingredients in a saucepan over low heat and whisk until smooth. Keep warm.

Filling and Decoration

1½ cups raspberry preserves
fresh raspberries
heavy cream

In a large clear bowl, arrange ⅓ of the cake cubes in a layer, spread ⅓ of the raspberry preserves over the cake in a thin layer, and drizzle with ⅓ of the fudge. Repeat process two more times, decoratively swirling fudge over final layer. Chill 4-6 hours.

Before serving, decorate top of the trifle with fresh raspberries. Serve with a pitcher of heavy cream. Serves 8 to 10.

Chocolate Truffle Cups

6 ounces semisweet chocolate chips

Melt chocolate in a double boiler or a bowl set over a pan of hot water. Stir until smooth.

Working quickly, use the back of a spoon or a small knife to spread chocolate on bottom and up sides of 7 to 8 paper cupcake liners. Set liners in a muffin pan. Chill until firm in freezer, 10-15 minutes. Carefully peel off the paper liners, handling chocolate as little as possible. (May be kept refrigerated up to 5 days.)

Mousse Filling

1⅓ cups whipping cream
⅔ cup confectioner's sugar, sifted
⅓ cup Dutch-process cocoa, sifted
1 teaspoon powdered instant coffee
2 teaspoons dark rum (optional)
confectioners' sugar or cocoa for decoration

Place cream, sugar, cocoa, instant coffee, and rum (if used) in large mixing bowl. Beat with electric mixer or whisk until cream forms soft peaks but is not stiff. Adjust flavoring to taste.

Spoon into small chocolate truffle cups and refrigerate until serving. Decorate tops with a dusting of confectioners' sugar or cocoa, if desired, just before serving.

Chutney Crescents

½ cup butter or margarine
3 ounces cream cheese
1 cup all-purpose flour, sifted
½ cup chutney
⅓ cup sugar
1 teaspoon ground cinnamon

Cream butter and cream cheese until smoothly blended. Beat in flour. Shape dough into smooth ball, wrap in waxed paper, and chill overnight.

Remove dough from refrigerator 30 minutes before using.

Preheat oven to 400° F. Roll dough to 1-inch thickness and cut with a 3-inch cookie cutter. Place small spoonful of chutney in center of each round. Fold over; press edges together. Bake on ungreased baking sheet for 15 minutes. Roll in sugar mixed with cinnamon.

Country Pâté

2 pounds bacon
½ cup chicken livers
2 tablespoons white wine
1 tablespoon butter
2 cloves garlic, minced
½ cup red onion, minced
½ cup cognac
½ cup ground turkey
½ cup Italian style pork sausage

3 tablespoons heavy cream
1 tablespoon Dijon mustard
2 eggs, lightly beaten
½ teaspoon salt
½ teaspoon pepper
1 teaspoon dried thyme
1 teaspoon dried sage
1 teaspoon ground allspice

Preheat oven to 350° F.

Place the bacon strips in a large pot of boiling water for 3 minutes. Drain and pat dry. Cover bottom and sides of a pâté or loaf pan with strips of bacon. Allow the strips of bacon to spill over the side generously. Reserve 6 strips of bacon for later use.

Mince remaining bacon and combine it with chicken livers and white wine in a blender. Blend on high speed until the mixture is smooth. Reserve.

Melt butter over low heat in a small pan. Stir in garlic and onion. Cook until tender. Pour onion, garlic, and butter into a large mixing bowl. Add cognac to the hot pan and reduce by half. Add to onion mixture.

Stir turkey, sausage, cream, mustard, eggs, salt, pepper, thyme, sage, and allspice into onion mixture. Mix well. Gently fold in liver mixture. Spoon a small amount of the mixture into a hot pan. Cook on both sides. Taste for flavor and texture.

Carefully fill bacon-lined pan with pâté mixture in stages, packing it down so there are no air holes. Top with protruding strips of bacon and reserved bacon strips. Place pâté in a warm water bath that reaches the half-way point of the pâté pan. Place in oven and bake for 2½ hours or until it has reached an internal temperature of 145° F. Remove from water bath.

Cool in refrigerator with a weight on top of the pan overnight. Slice and serve.

Mix remaining flour with all other ingredients. Spread mixture over hot crust. Return to oven for 25 minutes or until edges are lightly browned. Allow to cool completely before cutting into bars.

Cream Puff Swans

1 cup water
4 tablespoons unsalted butter
dash salt
1 cup flour
4 eggs

Preheat oven to 370° F.

Bring water, butter, and salt to boil in a saucepan. After butter has melted, add flour. Mix quickly with a wooden spoon until batter is smooth. Continue to stir for a few minutes over low heat to dry dough. Dough should not stick to your fingers when touched. Transfer dough to a clean bowl and let cool. Beat while adding eggs, one at a time, until mixture is smooth. Grease and flour a cookie sheet. Using about ¾ of the dough, drop large tablespoons of dough (2" diameter) onto the prepared sheet.

Place the remaining batter into a pastry tube fitted with a large round tip. Pipe the batter onto a prepared baking sheet in the shape of an "S". Brush all dough shapes with beaten egg and let dry for 25 minutes.

Bake for 30-35 minutes or until light brown. Turn off heat, open the oven door slightly, and let the puffs cool in the oven for 20 minutes. Cool completely before use.

Filling

2 cups   heavy cream
½   cup sugar
1 tablespoon cognac or vanilla

Cranberry Bars

¼ cup butter, room temperature
¼ cup brown sugar, packed
½ cup & 2 tablespoons all-purpose flour
1 egg
½ cup granulated sugar
1¼ cups dried cranberries and raisins, mixed
½ cup chopped walnuts
½ cup coconut
2 tablespoons orange juice or orange liqueur
1 tablespoon orange zest
1 teaspoon cinnamon
½ teaspoon vanilla
¼ teaspoon salt

Preheat oven to 375° F. Cream butter. Add brown sugar and ½ cup flour. Mix into a dough. Pat dough onto bottom of an 8" square baking pan. Bake for 5 minutes.

Whip the heavy cream until slightly thickened. Add sugar and continue whipping until the cream is thick. Fold in vanilla or cognac.

To assemble, split the puffs in half horizontally. Then split the top in half to make wings. Fill the bottom half with cream. Place an "S" shape in the cream for a neck and head. Add the wings. Refrigerate until ready to serve.

Currant and Orange Muffins

safflower oil to coat muffin tin
1 cup rice flour
1 tablespoon baking powder
1 teaspoon baking soda
½ cup rolled oats, ground
¼ cup honey
1 tablespoon maple syrup
¼ cup safflower oil
½ cup ground almonds
½ cup orange juice
1 teaspoon grated orange rind
2 eggs
½ cup dried currants

Preheat oven to 400° F. Lightly oil a 12-cup muffin tin.

In a large bowl combine rice flour, baking powder, baking soda, and ground oats. In a separate bowl combine honey, maple syrup, and the ¼ cup oil until very smooth. In a blender or food processor, puree almonds and orange juice, then strain. Add almond liquid to honey mixture along with orange rind.

Separate eggs. Stir yolks into honey mixture. Beat egg whites until stiff peaks form.
Combine dry and wet ingredients, then stir in currants. Fold in egg whites. Spoon into prepared muffin cups, filling each three fourths full. Bake until muffins spring back when pressed lightly in center (about 20 minutes). This healthy recipe contains no wheat, refined sugar, or milk.

Curry-Cheese Biscuits

2 cups all-purpose flour, sifted
½ teaspoon salt
½ teaspoon dry mustard
1½ teaspoons curry powder
pinch of cayenne pepper
⅔ cup butter
1 cup sharp cheddar cheese, grated
1 egg, beaten
2 tablespoons milk

Preheat oven to 400° F. Combine first 5 ingredients in a mixing bowl. Add butter and cut it into crumb consistency. Add cheese. Stir in beaten egg and milk.

Turn out onto a pastry board while still in the crumbly stage. Form into a mound with hands. Cut through the center of mound with a spatula. Stack half of the crumbly mound on the other half and again shape into a mound. Repeat this process until the dough holds together, about 10-12 times.

Roll into desired thickness. Cut with a 2-inch cookie cutter. Bake for 10 minutes.

Danish Puff

½ cup butter, softened
1 cup all-purpose flour
2 tablespoons water

Preheat oven to 350° F.

Cut butter into flour until particles are size of small peas. Sprinkle 2 tablespoons water over mixture and mix with fork until pastry forms a ball. Divide into halves and roll, or pat, each half into 12" x 13" rectangles. Place on an ungreased cookie sheet 3 inches apart. Set aside.

1 cup water
½ cup butter
1 teaspoon almond extract
1 cup all-purpose flour
3 eggs

In a saucepan, heat butter and water to a rolling boil. Remove from heat and quickly stir in almond extract and flour. Stir vigorously over low heat until mixture forms a ball - about 1 minute. Remove from heat. Add eggs and beat until smooth and glossy.

Spread half the mixture over one of the rectangles and repeat with the other half. Bake 1 hour or until topping has puffed, turned light brown and crisp. Remove from oven and allow to cool. (Topping will shrink and fall, forming the custard top).

Sugar Glaze

1½ cups confectioners' sugar
2 tablespoons butter, softened
1½ teaspoons vanilla
warm water

In a mixing bowl, combine all ingredients. Stir in warm water, 1 teaspoon at a time, until desired consistency is achieved. Drizzle sugar glaze over each and sprinkle with nuts if desired.

Deviled Crab Tart

2 sheets puff pastry
1 onion, chopped
2 cloves garlic, crushed
2 tablespoons mixed herbs
1 pound cream cheese, softened
4 tablespoons mustard
1 pound fresh crab meat
½ cup all-purpose flour
salt and pepper
1 egg, beaten
3 tablespoons fresh chopped dill

Preheat oven to 400° F.

Saute onion and garlic in small amount of oil. Remove from heat and add herbs.

Mix together cream cheese, mustard, crab, flour, and onion mixture until well blended. Add salt and pepper to taste.

Place 1 sheet of puff pastry into a greased 10" tart pan. Add crab mixture. Place puff pastry sheet on top. Crimp together with a fork.

Brush with beaten egg and sprinkle with some mixed herbs and dill. Cut a few slits into the top of the puff pastry. Bake for 20-25 minutes until well risen and golden brown.

Double Chocolate Brownies

1¼ cups all-purpose flour
¼ teaspoon soda
¼ teaspoon salt
½ cup butter
2 cups semi-sweet chocolate chips
3 eggs
1 teaspoon vanilla
1 cup sugar
⅓ cup chopped nuts

Preheat oven to 350° F. Grease a 13" x 9" x 2" baking pan. Combine flour, soda, and salt.

In a large saucepan over low heat, melt butter and half the chocolate chips, stirring until smooth. Remove from heat and allow to cool.

Stir in remaining chips and nuts. Spread into prepared pan. Bake 18-22 minutes. Cool completely. Cut into 24 brownies.

The Dunbar

Bar Base

1¾ cups all-purpose flour
1 cup sugar
6 ounces butter

Preheat oven to 350° F.

For the base, mix together flour, sugar and butter until well blended. Press mixture evenly into a 7 x 11-inch baking pan. Bake for 15 minutes or until light brown.

Filling

1 can condensed milk
8 ounces butter
4 tablespoons light corn syrup
1 cup sugar

Place all filling ingredients in medium saucepan and bring to a boil. Simmer, stirring constantly, for 5-8 minutes. The mixture will thicken and turn a light brown color. Pour the mixture over the cooked base and allow to cool completely.

Glaze

2 ounces milk chocolate, melted

Melt the chocolate and spread evenly over the top. Cool before cutting into slices.

Dundee Squares

1 cup sugar
2 cups all-purpose flour
8 ounces butter
1 large egg, beaten
1 teaspoon almond extract
1 cup raspberry jam
12 ounces semi-sweet chocolate chips
1 cup slivered almonds

Preheat oven to 350° F.

Grease and flour a 9 x 13-inch pan.

Combine sugar and flour in mixer. Add butter until mixture resembles fine breadcrumbs. Add beaten egg and almond extract until all ingredients are just moistened. Reserve 1 cup of this dough.

Press remaining dough into bottom of prepared pan. Spread jam over dough to within ½ inch of edge. Combine reserved cup of dough, chocolate chips, and almonds. Mix well. Sprinkle this mixture over jam, pressing lightly. Bake 35-40 minutes until golden brown. Cool slightly, then cut into squares.

Earl Grey Crème Brûlée

1½ quarts heavy cream
5 whole large eggs, slightly beaten
5 large egg yolks, slightly beaten
1½ cups brown sugar
1 cup white sugar
1 cup Earl Grey tea, strongly brewed

Preheat oven to 350° F. Place heavy cream, slightly beaten eggs, egg yolks, and sugars in top of double boiler. Cook over medium heat, stirring frequently until slightly thickened. Add tea and pour into small ramekins. Bake until set, approximately 50 - 60 minutes. Custard is done when knife stuck in center comes out clean. Cool to room temperature and refrigerate overnight.

Mix a small amount of brown sugar and white sugar together. Pat lightly on top of custard and then torch until sugar melts. Serve immediately.

Egg & Cress Tea Sandwiches

3 medium eggs
2 teaspoons mayonnaise
Dash salt
Dash pepper
6-8 slices bread
2 ounces butter, room temperature
2 bunches fresh watercress

Boil eggs for 8 minutes. Drain and run under cold water to stop cooking process. Shell eggs and mash with a fork until finely chopped. Add mayonnaise, salt, pepper and blend thoroughly.

Spread bread lightly with butter. Spread egg mayonnaise generously over half the slices of bread and top with watercress. Press buttered slices on top. Trim off crusts and cut into triangles or squares.

Empress Lemon Tarts

1 cup lemon juice
zest of 1 lemon
1½ cups sugar
6 eggs
1⅔ cups double cream
8 pre-baked tart shells

Preheat oven to 300° F.

Combine lemon juice, zest, and sugar. Whisk in eggs and cream. Spoon mixture into pre-baked tart shells. Bake for 25 minutes. Sprinkle with granulated sugar and place under a broiler until caramelized. Serve with a dollop of whipped cream.

Fruit Tarts

2 cups all-purpose flour
Dash salt
½ teaspoon sugar
1½ sticks unsalted butter, chilled & chopped
2-3 tablespoons ice water

In a bowl, combine flour, salt, sugar, and butter. Mix at low speed for about 8 minutes or until mixture is consistency of fine cornmeal.

Add up to 3 tablespoons of water. The pastry will roll from sides of bowl.

Remove pastry to a lightly floured surface and shape into ball. Cover with waxed paper and chill for 30-45 minutes.

Preheat oven to 450° F.

Roll chilled dough to desired thickness. Cut circles with a 2-inch cutter and line each muffin cup with a circle. Bake 8 minutes or until golden.

Crème Anglaise Filling

3 egg yolks
½ cup sugar
1 tablespoon cornstarch
1 cup milk
¼ teaspoon vanilla
fresh strawberries or raspberries

In a double boiler, heat egg yolks and sugar. Stir constantly with a whisk until the mixture turns to ribbons.

Dissolve cornstarch in milk. Add to egg mixture. Add vanilla and mix until thick. Remove from heat and place on ice. Stir until cold. Cover.

Fill each tart with Crème Anglaise and top with fruit.

Fruit Glaze

Mix 2 tablespoons red currant jelly and 1 teaspoon water. Use a brush to paint the fruit topping.

Green Tea Smoothies

1½ teaspoons powdered green tea
1½ cups low fat yogurt
2 medium ripe peaches, pitted and chunked
  (mangos, apricots or bananas may be substituted)
1-3 teaspoons honey
6 ice cubes

Place all ingredients in a blender and puree until completely blended.

Serve immediately in a tall glass.

Homestead Cookies

½ cup butter, room temperature
½ cup granulated sugar
½ cup light brown sugar
1 egg
1 teaspoon vanilla
1 cup all-purpose flour
2 cups rolled oats
½ teaspoon baking powder
½ teaspoon baking soda
½ teaspoon salt
1 cup apples, chopped fine

Preheat oven to 375° F.

Line baking sheets with parchment or grease lightly.

In a large bowl, cream together butter, granulated sugar, and brown sugar until light and fluffy. Beat in egg and vanilla.

In another bowl, stir together flour, oats, baking powder, baking soda, and salt. Gradually mix dry ingredients into butter mixture. Stir in apples.

Drop a tablespoon of dough onto prepared baking sheets, leaving 1½ inches between them.

Bake 8 to 10 minutes or until light golden. Cool on wire racks and store in airtight container.

Iced Matcha Cappuccino

1 teaspoon matcha green tea
2 teaspoons sugar
⅔ cup 190° F water
ice cubes

Whisk dry matcha, sugar, and hot water until frothy. Pour into a tall glass of ice.

Key West Poached Salmon

1¼ pounds fresh salmon filet, skin attached
1½ cups key lime vinaigrette (purchased)
dried dill
1½ teaspoon cornstarch
1 tablespoon sugar
salad greens

Place salmon filet in glass dish and spoon ½ cup of key lime vinaigrette over filet. Marinate for at least one hour.

Preheat oven to 350° F. Wrap marinated salmon in a foil pouch and bake for approximately 20 minutes. Salmon is done when it flakes easily. Sprinkle lightly with dried dill.

Add cornstarch and sugar to remaining key lime vinaigrette. Heat in small saucepan until slightly thickened. Pour over salmon, and bake uncovered for 5 minutes. This glazes the salmon.

Refrigerate until completely cold. Cut into equal wedges. Remove skin. Place over greens and garnish as desired. Serve with key lime vinaigrette.

Lapsang Souchong Chicken Salad

3 pounds boneless chicken breast
3 quarts water
¼ cup Lapsang Souchong loose leaf tea
¼ cup soy sauce
1 ounce ginger root, chopped
1 large apple, chopped
2 garlic cloves, chopped
2 tablespoons chopped red bell pepper
2 tablespoons chopped yellow bell pepper
2 cups mayonnaise
½ teaspoon salt
1 teaspoon white pepper

Trim any fat from chicken, and cut chicken breasts into halves. Combine chicken and enough water to cover in a 5 quart saucepan. Add tea and soy sauce. Bring to a boil; reduce heat to just below the boiling point. Poach for 30 minutes or until chicken is cooked through. Let stand to cool. Drain and rinse chicken and cut into medium chunks.

Combine ginger root, apple, garlic, red pepper, and yellow pepper in a bowl. Add mayonnaise and mix well. Stir in chicken. Season with salt and white pepper. Serve on toasted wheat bread.

Lemon Cake

½ cup butter
1 cup sugar
2 eggs
1½ cups all-purpose flour
1 teaspoon baking powder
pinch of salt
1 cup milk
1 lemon, juice and grated rind

Preheat oven to 300° F.

Cream butter and sugar. Add eggs. Sift together flour, baking powder, and salt. Add to butter mixture, alternately with the milk. Mix well. Add lemon juice and grated rind.

Bake in a greased loaf pan for 1 hour and 10 minutes.

Lemon Glaze

½ lemon
¼ cup confectioners' sugar

Juice the half lemon and mix with sugar. Add more juice if needed.
Pierce the top of the cake in several places. Pour lemon glaze over it. Allow to cool, slice, and serve.

Lemon Curd

3 eggs
½ cup fresh lemon juice
½ cup unsalted butter, melted
1 cup sugar

In the top of a double boiler, beat eggs until frothy. Stir in lemon juice, sugar and melted butter. Place over simmering water. Stir constantly for 20 minutes. The mixture should become slightly thickened.

Remove from heat and spoon into a pint-sized container. Cool to room temperature, cover and refrigerate at least two hours before serving. Keeps well for two weeks.

Lemon Meringues

3 egg whites
½ teaspoon cream of tartar
1 cup sugar
Pinch salt
½ teaspoon vanilla

Place egg whites in mixing bowl. Using whisk attachment, add cream of tartar and beat on high speed. Mix until frothy. Add sugar and salt a little at a time. Add vanilla. Continue to whip until stiff peaks form.

Preheat oven to 200° F. Line a baking sheet with parchment paper. Spoon or pipe a "bird's nest" of meringue, 1-2 inches in circumference.
Place in oven for 1 hour (check to make sure they do not brown).

Turn oven off and leave an additional two hours or overnight.

When dry and cool, fill with lemon curd.

Lemon Poppy Seed Loaf

½ pound butter, unsalted
1½ cups sugar
2 eggs, large
2 cups all-purpose flour
2 teaspoons baking powder
1 cup 2% milk
1 teaspoon salt
2 lemons, zest only
3 tablespoons poppy seeds

Preheat oven to 350° F. Cream butter and sugar together in a bowl. Add eggs slowly, one at a time. Scrape down bowl. Add dry ingredients and then wet ingredients, scraping bowl well. Add poppy seeds and lemon zest. Mix lightly. In a lightly greased loaf pan bake for 30-35 minutes or until golden brown. Let cool.

Lemon Syrup

2 lemons, juiced
6 tablespoons sugar
6 tablespoons water

In a sauce pan, combine lemon juice, sugar, and water. Reduce over low heat until thick in consistency. Pour over loaves.

Lemon Squares

1 cup all-purpose flour
¼ cup confectioners' sugar
1 stick butter or margarine

Preheat oven to 350° F.

Cut flour and sugar into butter so that it resembles coarse meal. Press firmly into an 8 or 9-inch pan. Bake 15 minutes or until slightly brown.

Topping

2 eggs
1 cup granulated sugar
½ teaspoon baking powder
2 tablespoons lemon juice with grated rind

Mix ingredients well and pour over the top of the baked crust. Bake 20 minutes more at 350° F. Cut into squares while warm and sprinkle thickly with confectioners' sugar.

Lime Meltaways

¾ cup butter, room temperature
⅓ cup powdered sugar
2 limes, zested
1¾ cups all-purpose flour
2 tablespoons cornstarch
¼ teaspoon salt
1 tablespoon vanilla
2 tablespoons lime juice

Preheat oven to 350° F. Cream together butter, powdered sugar and zest. Sift flour, cornstarch, and salt together.

Combine all ingredients to form a stiff dough. Form into logs approximately the diameter of a half dollar and freeze. Slice when needed. Bake for 10-12 minutes. Cool and roll in powdered sugar.

Macaroons

¼ cup confectioners' sugar, sifted
1 cup powdered sugar
1 cup ground almonds
3 egg whites
⅛ teaspoon almond extract
powdered sugar for dusting
35-40 whole blanched almonds

Preheat oven to 300° F. Line two baking sheets with parchment paper.

In a large bowl, mix sugars and ground almonds. Make a well in the center and drop in one egg white. Using a fork, work egg white into sugar mixture until a stiff, smooth paste is formed. Gradually work in remaining egg whites until paste is soft and smooth. Add almond flavoring.

Put mixture into a piping bag fitted with a medium star nozzle. Pipe about 10 small macaroons on each baking sheet. Extra mixture may be refrigerated until ready to cook the next batch.

Dust each macaroon with confectioners' sugar and top with an almond. Bake for 30 minutes or until firm and golden. Remove from oven and slide parchment paper and macaroons on a wire rack. Leave to cool completely.

Re-line the baking sheets and pipe and bake the remaining mixture.When the macaroons are cool, remove them from the paper.

Madeleines

1¼ cups sifted cake flour
½ teaspoon baking powder
¼ teaspoon salt
3 eggs
1 teaspoon vanilla
⅔ cup sugar
2 teaspoons lemon rind, finely grated
¾ cup unsalted butter, melted and cooled
confectioners' sugar for dusting

Preheat oven to 350° F.

Sift together flour, baking powder, and salt.

Beat eggs until light. Add vanilla and gradually beat in sugar, a little at a time. Continue beating until volume has increased about four times the original. Fold in lemon rind. Gradually fold in flour mixture. Stir in melted and cooled butter.

Brush pans with additional melted butter. Spoon 1 tablespoon batter into each shell to about ¾ full.

Bake for 12-15 minutes or until golden brown. Remove from pan and dust with confectioners' sugar.

Mint Butter

2 cups sweet butter, softened
1 cup mint leaves, rinsed
1 teaspoon lemon juice
1 teaspoon salt
1 teaspoon sugar

Using a food processor, make a purée of all ingredients. Rub through a fine sieve if desired. Spoon into plastic containers and chill until needed. (May be frozen.)

Allow butter to come to room temperature before using. Serve with warm scones or spread over a toasted English muffin.

Miso Pumpkin Soup

4 quarts hot water
3 parsnips, peeled & diced
1 large sweet potato, peeled & diced
1 3-inch sheet kombu (seaweed)
13 ounces yellow miso
5 cups pureed pumpkin
3 tablespoons fresh ginger, grated
1 cup mirin (Japanese cooking wine)
¼ cup soy sauce
scallions, chopped for garnish
ground nutmeg

In a medium saucepan, bring 1 quart water to boil. Add parsnips and potato. Bring to boil for 15 minutes.

In a small saucepan, soak kombu in hot water for about 5 minutes.

In a large soup pot, combine 3 quarts of water, miso and pumpkin. Adjust heat to low setting.

Drain parsnips and potato. Add to soup. Add kombu, ginger, mirin, and soy sauce. Simmer for 30 minutes. Pour into individual bowls and garnish with scallions and a dash of nutmeg.

Miss Mable's Cookie Jar Tea Cakes

⅔ cup shortening
¾ cup sugar
1 egg
½ teaspoon vanilla
½ teaspoon salt
2 cups all-purpose flour, sifted
1½ teaspoons baking powder
2 tablespoons milk

Preheat oven to 375° F. Cream shortening and sugar. Add egg. Beat mixture until light and fluffy. Add vanilla.

Sift together dry ingredients and stir into creamed mixture along with milk. Divide dough in half and chill for 1 hour. Roll dough out to ⅛ inch. Cut with a favorite cookie cutter.

Place on a greased cookie sheet and bake for about 10 minutes or until light brown. Makes about 2 dozen medium tea cakes.

Mother Hubbard's Squash Soup

2 large winter squash
2 medium yellow onions
1 large leek
1 tablespoon garlic
1½ quarts chicken stock
1 quart cream
4 ounces butter
salt and pepper to taste

Split squash and remove seeds. Bake at 350° F until soft (pierces easily with knife). Set aside. Melt 2 ounces butter in sauce pan and sauté onion, leek, and garlic until translucent. Add chicken stock. Cook until hot. Add squash.

In another pan, reduce cream by half and add to soup. Add remaining butter to soup and blend in a blender. Season with salt and pepper. Serve hot.

Oriental Chicken Salad

1 head Napa cabbage
2 green lettuce leaves
1 carrot, coarsely grated
4-5 cups cooked chicken breast, diced

Slice cabbage and lettuce finely. Combine with carrot and diced chicken.

1 package Ramen noodles
20 ounces slivered almonds
¼ cup sesame seeds
⅓ stick butter

Discard the Ramen noodles flavor packet. Crush the noodles well in unopened bag. Melt the butter in a skillet over medium heat. Fry the noodles, almonds, and sesame seeds until golden brown. Stir constantly to avoid burning.

Dressing

1 packet *Good Seasonings* Oriental Sesame Dressing
2 tablespoons sugar

Make dressing according to package directions. Add sugar.

Put all ingredients together and just before serving, toss generously with dressing to taste.

Passion Fruit Roulade

1½ cups sugar
1 cup all-purpose flour
1 teaspoon baking soda
1 teaspoon baking powder
½ teaspoon salt
6 large egg yolks
½ cup vegetable oil
½ cup water
2 tablespoons vanilla
6 large egg whites

Preheat oven to 350° F. Spray a sheet pan with cooking spray, line with parchment paper and spray again lightly.

Sift together 1 cup sugar, flour, soda, and baking powder. Add salt. In a bowl, combine the yolks, oil, water, and vanilla. Gradually add dry ingredients. Set aside.

Beat 6 egg whites and add remaining ½ cup sugar. Fold about ½ whites into dough mixture to lighten. Gradually add remaining whites. Pour into prepared pan and bake 10-12 minutes.

Remove and cool on a rack.

Filling

1½ cups whipping cream
⅓ cup confectioners' sugar, sifted
1½ teaspoon unflavored gelatin
4 tablespoons cold water
¼ cup passion fruit concentrate (frozen fruit juice reduced by half by boiling)

Dissolve gelatin in cold water and allow to bloom. Place over hot water until melted. Allow to cool just until tepid, but not cool. Beat cream until foamy. Slowly add confectioners' sugar and whip until soft peaks are reached. Add cool gelatin and passion fruit. Continue to whip until fairly stiff.

Spread towel on counter and sprinkle with sifted confectioners' sugar. Turn cake on a towel and remove paper.

Spread filling onto cake, leaving about 1 inch on one long edge. Roll cake and filling, using towel to assist with rolling, moving towards the uncoated edge. Place on tray and refrigerate several hours.

Frosting

4 cups confectioners' sugar, sifted
¼ cup passion fruit concentrate
2 tablespoons heavy cream

Combine 3½ cups sugar with passion fruit and cream. Add remaining sugar as needed. Spread onto cake.

117

Perkins

2 cups all-purpose flour
1⅓ cups oatmeal
1 cup sugar
½ teaspoon baking soda
2½ teaspoons ginger
½ teaspoon nutmeg
½ teaspoon allspice
½ teaspoon cinnamon
4 ounces butter
1 egg, beaten
6 teaspoons light corn syrup

Preheat oven to 350° F. Grease a baking sheet. Combine dry ingredients. With your fingers, work in the butter until it resembles breadcrumbs, or mix in a food processor. Add beaten egg and syrup. Form dough into golf-ball size shapes. Put an almond on each and flatten slightly.

Bake about 15 minutes. Makes 30 cookies.

Phyllo Pastries with Smoked Turkey and Mushrooms

1 cup mushrooms, minced
2 cloves garlic, minced
¼ cup onion, minced
¼ cup sherry
1 teaspoon olive oil
3 tablespoons chopped parsley
½ cup crumbled feta cheese
¼ cup grated low-fat mozzarella cheese
¼ teaspoon dried oregano
¼ teaspoon dried thyme
¼ pound finely minced smoked turkey, trimmed of fat
15 sheets phyllo dough
⅓ cup unsalted butter, melted

In a large skillet over medium high heat, sauté mushrooms, garlic, and onion in sherry and olive oil until soft. Add parsley, feta, mozzarella, oregano, thyme, and turkey. Remove from heat.

Preheat oven to 350° F. Lightly oil two 9x12-inch baking sheets.

Lay phyllo dough on a clean, dry surface. Cut each sheet in half widthwise to make 30 smaller sheets. Stack them evenly on top of each other, and cover with a piece of plastic wrap and a slightly dampened dish towel as you do the next step.

Butter 1 sheet and cut into 3 long strips. Lay the 3 strips on top of each other. Place about 2 tablespoons of filling in the lower right section near the edge. Fold bottom right corner of phyllo over filling to meet left edge, creating a small triangle. Continue folding pastry, as you would a flag, until you reach the top. You will end up with a triangle-shaped pastry.

Lightly butter top of filled triangle and place on prepared baking sheet. Repeat process until all the filling has been used. Bake pastries 20 minutes or until golden. Serve warm.

Potted Crab Crostini

2 pounds jumbo lump crab
1 orange
4 ounces dry sherry
4 ounces unsalted butter
½ teaspoon salt
½ teaspoon fresh ground black pepper
3 drops Tabasco
baguette crostini
½ cup clarified butter (optional)

Preheat oven to 425° F. Zest and juice the orange. In a small sauce pan, place orange zest, orange juice, and sherry. Simmer and reduce by half. Strain mixture through a cheese cloth.
In a food processor, beat butter and orange reduction until smooth, then add crab. Continue to blend as you add salt, pepper, and Tabasco.

When smooth, remove to a piping bag with a #10 tip. Slice baguettes into ¼-inch thick diagonal slices. Spray with clarified butter (or baking spray) and toast on a sheet pan in a hot oven until brown.

Pipe potted crab on crostini and drizzle with a tiny bit of clarified butter.

Praline Pecan Kisses

1 cup light brown sugar
1 egg white, beaten stiff
1½ cups pecan halves

Preheat oven to 250° F. Line a cookie sheet with aluminum foil.

Beat egg white until stiff peaks form. Gradually add sugar. Fold in pecans. Drop teaspoon mounds on aluminum foil. Bake 30 - 35 minutes. Allow to cool.

Pumpkin Scones

4 ½ cups all-purpose flour
5 teaspoons baking powder
1 teaspoon cinnamon
½ teaspoon nutmeg
1 teaspoon salt
½ cup light brown sugar
½ cup unsalted butter, softened
2 cups canned pumpkin puree
1⅓ cups milk
2 cups pecans, chopped

Preheat oven to 375° F. Prepare two large baking sheets with cooking spray.

In a large mixing bowl, combine dry ingredients. Cut in butter until it resembles coarse meal. Add pumpkin, milk and nuts. Stir until well mixed. Using a ½ cup measure, scoop batter into small rounds on the baking sheets. Leave a 2" space between each scone.

Bake for 12 to 15 minutes, until the edges begin to brown. Remove to a cooling rack. Makes 30.

Queen Mother's Cake

1 cup boiling water
8 ounces chopped, pitted dates
1 teaspoon baking soda
3 ounces butter
1 cup sugar
1 egg, beaten
1 teaspoon vanilla
1 teaspoon salt
1 teaspoon baking powder
2 cups flour
2 ounces chopped walnuts

Preheat oven to 350° F. Grease and flour an 8" square cake pan.

Pour boiling water over chopped dates; add baking soda and set aside. Beat butter and sugar together until light and fluffy; add egg and vanilla. Mix in salt, baking powder, and flour until well blended. Add walnuts and date mixture, and mix for 1-2 minutes longer. Bake for 50-60 minutes. Cool completely.

Topping

2 tablespoons brown sugar
2 tablespoons butter
2 tablespoons heavy cream
Chopped walnuts

In a medium saucepan, mix topping ingredients together. Bring to a boil. Simmer for 3 minutes only, stirring occasionally. Pour over cake and sprinkle with chopped walnuts.

Roasted Vegetable and Asiago Quiche

2 carrots, peeled
15 mushrooms
1 tomato, quartered
6 garlic cloves
2 red peppers
1 onion
½ cup olive oil
Pinch salt
Pinch black pepper
1 cup Asiago cheese

Preheat oven to 400° F.

Cut all vegetables into medium dice. Toss with olive oil, salt and pepper. Place in a heat proof dish and roast in oven for 20-30 minutes or until the vegetables are caramelized. Cool vegetables and finely chop.

Quiche Cream

8 eggs, large
1 cup whipping cream
Pinch nutmeg
12 3-inch tart shells

Prebake quiche shells according to package directions. In a bowl, whisk eggs, cream, and nutmeg together. Add grated Asiago cheese.

Heat oven to 350° F. Spoon vegetable mix into baked shells and cover with quiche cream. Bake at for 15 -25 minutes or until set in the middle.

Sally Lunns

1 cup milk
¼ cup sugar
2 teaspoons salt
1 stick butter
½ cup very warm water
1 package dry yeast
3 eggs
4 - 4½ cups all-purpose flour

Scald the milk. Add sugar, salt, and butter. Cool to lukewarm.

Dissolve yeast in the warm water in a large bowl. Add lukewarm milk mixture, eggs, and flour. Beat until smooth. Cover and allow to rise for 1 hour.

Preheat oven to 350° F.

Stir dough again and pour into a large, prepared loaf pan. Let rise for 30 minutes in a warm, draft-free area.

Bake for 40 minutes or until crusty and brown. Remove from pan to rack. Brush with butter. Serve warm or toasted with butter and preserves.

Scones with Currants

2 cups all-purpose flour
2 teaspoons baking powder
½ teaspoon salt
¼ teaspoon baking soda
6 tablespoons unsalted cold butter
½ cup currants
½ cup buttermilk
1 egg
1 tablespoon cream
1 tablespoon sugar

Preheat oven to 400° F. Lightly grease a large baking sheet. Combine flour, baking powder, salt, and soda. With a pastry blender, cut in butter, mixing until mixture resembles coarse crumbs. Mix in currants.

Whisk buttermilk and egg together, then add to flour mixture. Stir together until a soft ball of dough forms. Turn onto a lightly floured surface and knead gently, turning five or six times.

Roll out dough with a floured rolling pin to about ½ inch thickness. Cut out scones and place on the baking sheet. Brush the tops lightly with cream and sprinkle with sugar. Bake 10 to 12 minutes or until light brown.

Salmon and Dill Sandwiches

8 ounces cream cheese, room temperature
heavy cream
1 teaspoon dill weed, fresh or dried
1 loaf bread, thinly sliced and buttered
16 slices smoked salmon, thinly sliced
fresh dill or parsley for garnish

In a bowl, beat cream cheese, then thin with cream. Mix in dill.

Spread mixture on bread. Add a very thin slice of salmon. Trim crusts, slice into triangles, and garnish with dill or parsley.

Scotch Whisky Balls

2 cups gingersnap cookies, finely ground
1 cup pecans, finely ground
¼ cup Scotch whisky
3 tablespoons corn syrup
1½ cups powdered sugar, sifted

In a mixing bowl, combine cookie crumbs, nuts, whisky, corn syrup, and 1 cup powdered sugar. Mix thoroughly with a wooden spoon. Form into small balls.

Roll each ball in powdered sugar. Make ahead and chill for future use.

Sour Cherry Bakewell Slices

1¼ cups butter
1¼ cups sugar
2 cups almond paste
9 eggs
¼ cup all-purpose flour
1 teaspoon baking powder
¾ cup canned sour cherries (drained)
¼ cup sliced almonds

Preheat oven to 325° F.

Grease and line a round cake pan. Combine butter, sugar, and almond paste. Cream until smooth. Slowly add eggs. Fold in flour and baking powder. Add sour cherries and mix.

Pour into prepared pan and sprinkle with almonds. Bake 45 minutes. Allow to cool before slicing.

Sticky Toffee Pudding

4 ounces butter, softened
6 ounces dark brown sugar
4 eggs, slightly beaten
8 ounces self-rising flour
1 teaspoon baking soda
2 tablespoons strong coffee with some grounds
8 ounces dates, pitted and chopped
1 cup boiling water

Preheat oven to 350° F.

Line a 9" square or round cake pan with double parchment paper.

Cream together brown sugar and butter until smooth. Add eggs one at a time, mixing thoroughly after each addition. Fold in flour (in three sessions) until smooth.

Place the chopped dates in a medium size mixing bowl. Mix baking soda and coffee in a separate small bowl. Pour over dates. Add boiling water. Stir and let cool slightly.

Fold into batter until thoroughly blended. Pour into prepared pan.

Bake for 1½ hours or until springy to the touch. Let cool and top with hot caramel sauce.

Caramel Sauce

8 tablespoons brown sugar
4 tablespoons heavy cream
2 tablespoons butter

In a saucepan, bring to a boil while stirring.

Pour over cake. Place immediately under the broiler until sauce bubbles, no more than ten minutes.

Serve warm with a topping of freshly prepared whipped cream.

Strawberry Rhubarb Cake

3 cups rhubarb
1 cup strawberries, quartered
2 envelopes unflavored gelatin
½ cup superfine sugar

Grease a 9" x 13" baking dish. In a bowl, combine fruit, gelatin and sugar. Set aside.

¼ cup all-purpose flour
½ cup sugar
½ cup butter

In another bowl, cut butter into flour and sugar until crumbly. Set aside.

Cake batter

½ cup butter
1½ cups sugar
2 eggs
3 cups cake flour
4 teaspoons baking powder
pinch salt
1 cup milk
1 teaspoon vanilla

Preheat oven to 350° F.

Cream butter and sugar until light and fluffy. Add eggs and beat until fully blended.

Combine flour, baking powder and salt. To the creamed mixture, add ⅓ of the dry ingredients. Blend well. Add ⅓ of the milk and blend. Repeat with another ⅓ of dry, then milk. When adding the last ⅓ milk, add vanilla. Beat until blended. Pour batter into prepared pan, spreading evenly.

Top with the fruit, then the crumble. Bake for 35-40 minutes or until inserted skewer comes out clean. Serve with cream poured over the top or with clotted cream on the side

Summery Zucchini-Pistachio Tea Bread

1½ cups all-purpose flour
1½ teaspoons baking soda
¼ teaspoon ground cinnamon
¾ cup sugar
2 large eggs
½ cup vegetable oil
1 teaspoon vanilla
½ teaspoon salt
1½ cups toasted shelled pistachio nuts
1½ cups grated zucchini, squeezed dry

Preheat oven to 350° F.

Sift together flour, baking soda, and cinnamon.

In a second bowl, whisk together sugar, eggs, vegetable oil, vanilla, and salt. Add to the dry ingredients and stir until combined. Fold in zucchini and nuts.

Transfer batter to a well-buttered 5" x 9" loaf pan and bake for 50-60 minutes or until a cake tester inserted in the center comes out clean.

Let cool in the pan on a rack for 10 minutes. Invert onto rack and cool completely.

Frosting

1 large egg
¾ cup sugar
2½ tablespoons cold water
⅛ teaspoon cream of tartar
¾ teaspoon light corn syrup
½ teaspoon vanilla

In a double boiler over simmering water, combine all ingredients except vanilla. Using a hand mixer, beat the mixture for 7 minutes or until thick and fluffy. Beat in the vanilla. Frost top of cake and allow frosting to set before serving.

Sun Dried Tomato and Walnut Potatoes

1½ pounds red skinned boiling potatoes
15 sundried tomato halves (not packed in oil)
1 teaspoon dried rosemary
2 cloves garlic
½ cup fat-free mayonnaise
⅓ cup cottage cheese
1 tablespoon lemon juice
¾ cup chopped walnuts
salt to taste
pepper to taste

Steam potatoes. Cool to room temperature and slice in half. Hollow out 1 tablespoon from each center.

Cover tomato halves with boiling water and soak for 10 minutes. Drain and pat dry tomatoes. Place in food processor with rosemary and garlic. Process until coarsely chopped. Add mayonnaise, cottage cheese, and lemon juice. Process until smooth. Add walnuts and process until incorporated. Season with salt and pepper. Yields 1½ cups of tomato filling.

Spoon 1 tablespoon of tomato filling into each potato half. Serve at room temperature.

Tea House Gingerbread

1⅓ cups canola oil
3 medium eggs
⅓ cup honey
⅓ cup molasses
⅓ cup sugar
3½ cups all-purpose flour
2 teaspoons baking powder
⅔ teaspoon powdered ginger
⅔ teaspoon cinnamon
1⅓ cup brewed black tea

Preheat oven to 400° F.

In a large bowl, mix oil, eggs, honey, molasses, and sugar. Beat at medium speed, scraping often, until creamy. Reduce to low speed and add tea. Mix well. Sift together dry ingredients. Add dry ingredients to wet mixture. Mix until moistened.

Pour into oiled and floured baking pans. Bake 35-40 minutes or until set.

Tea Seared Tuna

1 cup hojicha (roasted Japanese green tea)
1 tablespoon kosher or sea salt
½ tablespoon coarsely ground black pepper
4-6 ahi tuna fillets
⅓ cup canola oil
1 tablespoon sesame oil

In a food processor, prepare the tea rub by blending tea, salt and pepper. Mixture should be coarse.

Soak tuna fillets in ice cold water for 2 to 3 minutes. Remove from water and pat dry with a paper towel. Coat each fillet with tea rub.

In a skillet, heat oils until sizzling. Sear fillets for 2 to 3 minutes on each side. Remove from heat. Slice thin for serving with wasabi mayonnaise.

Wasabi Mayonnaise

1 tablespoon dry wasabi powder
1 cup mayonnaise
1 teaspoon water

Whisk all ingredients together in a small bowl. Serve as an accompaniment to the sliced tuna.

This dish can be made in advance and served cold. Do not slice until ready to serve or the tuna will dry out.

Thumbprint Cookies

4 ounces butter, softened
1 cup shortening
1 cup brown sugar
2½ teaspoons vanilla
4 egg yolks
4 cups all-purpose flour
¾ teaspoon salt
4 egg whites, beaten
¼ cup hazelnuts, chopped fine
1 small jar raspberry or apricot preserves

Preheat oven to 350° F. Cream together butter, shortening, brown sugar, and vanilla. Add yolks, one at a time. Add flour and salt. Mix until just combined.

Place scoops of dough onto a baking sheet, then flatten. Coat top with egg whites and lightly sprinkle with hazelnuts. Bake 15 minutes or until firm.

Remove from oven and make a thumbprint in the center of each cookie while still warm. Fill with preserves. Allow to cool before serving.

Toffee Bars

4 ounces butter, room temperature
4 ounces light brown sugar
1 egg yolk
⅓ cup all-purpose flour
1 cup oats

Preheat oven to 375° F. Grease a 7"x11" Swiss roll or tart pan. Beat together butter, sugar, and egg yolk until light and smooth. Add flour and oats and mix well. Press into prepared pan. Bake 15-20 minutes. Cool slightly in pan.

Topping

3 ounces chocolate
1 ounce butter
1 cup chopped walnuts or almonds

Melt chocolate and butter together. Spread over warm cake. Top with nuts and allow topping to set. While still warm, cut into bars and allow to completely cool before storing in a closed tin.

Truffles

1 cup cream
3 tablespoons Grand Marnier or Kahlua
6 ounces semi-sweet chocolate
6 ounces sweet chocolate
8 tablespoons unsalted butter, softened
confectioners' sugar
unsweetened Dutch process powdered cocoa

Bring cream to a boil and reduce to ½ cup. Add liqueur and chocolate. Stir over low heat until chocolate melts. Whisk in soft butter and mix until smooth. Pour into a bowl and refrigerate until firm.

Use a small melon scoop to shape the chocolate mixture into balls. Roll half of each ball in confectioners' sugar and half in cocoa. Line a covered tin or plastic container with wax paper and store truffles in refrigerator. Makes 50.

Vanilla Butterscotch Bread

3 cups all-purpose flour, sifted
1¼ teaspoons baking powder
¾ teaspoon salt
¾ teaspoon baking soda
2 eggs, beaten
1½ cups light brown sugar
⅓ cup butter or margarine, melted
1½ teaspoons vanilla
¾ cup chopped pecans or walnuts
1½ cups buttermilk

Preheat oven to 350° F. Sift together first 4 ingredients and set aside.

Beat eggs in a mixing bowl. Gradually blend in sugar. Add butter and vanilla. Stir in nuts. Add flour mixture alternately with milk, mixing only enough to blend the ingredients.

Pour into a well-greased, lightly floured 9" x 5" x 3"-inch loaf pan. Bake for 1 hour or until done.

Cool in pan for 10 minutes. Turn onto a wire rack to finish cooling. This bread cuts better if made the day before it is to be eaten.

Victorian Sponge

4 ounces butter, room temperature
½ cup granulated sugar
2 medium eggs, beaten
1 cup self-rising flour
1 tablespoon boiling water
⅓ cup raspberry jam
1 tablespoon confectioners' sugar

Preheat oven to 350° F.

Grease and line two 7" round cake pans.

With an electric mixer, cream butter and sugar together until light and fluffy. Beat in eggs, a little at a time, alternating with 1 tablespoon of flour between each addition. Beat thoroughly.

Fold in remaining flour with a metal spoon. Stir in boiling water and mix well.

Divide mixture between the prepared pans and bake for 20-25 minutes or until the cake is lightly browned and springs back when pressed lightly with your finger. Remove from the oven and place on a wire rack to cool.

When cold, spread the underside of one cake with jam. Lay the other cake carefully on top. Cover lightly with sifted confectioners' sugar.

Although raspberry jam is the most common filling for a classic Victorian Sponge, lemon or raspberry curd also makes a delicious filling between the layered cakes.

Waldorf Celery Boats

2 stalks fresh crisp celery
½ cup blue cheese, crumbled
¼ cup finely chopped toasted walnuts
½ cup finely chopped red delicious apple
1 teaspoon lemon juice
leaf lettuce

Cut celery into 1½ inch bite-size pieces. In a medium bowl, combine blue cheese and walnuts. In a small bowl, mix the lemon juice with the chopped apple. Drain off any excess juice.

Add apple to the cheese mixture. Gently mix together.

Place a small amount of mixture into each piece of celery. Place each celery boat on top of a piece of leaf lettuce and serve. Serves 16.

Warm Chocolate Pudding Cakes

12 ounces bittersweet chocolate
1 cup butter

Place chocolate and butter into a small saucepan. Warm over low heat until melted. Set aside.

Prepare 6 ramekins by lightly buttering the interiors. Preheat oven to 350° F.

1 cup sugar
½ cup all-purpose flour
6 eggs

Combine sugar and flour in a large mixing bowl. Add eggs, one at a time, and beat together until fluffy, about 5 minutes. Add chocolate until mixed thoroughly. Pour into 6 prepared ramekins. Bake for 15 minutes. Serve warm.

White Chocolate Almond Cakes

½ pound almond paste
½ cup sugar
3 eggs
lemon zest
⅓ cup all-purpose flour
4 ounces butter
8 ounces white chocolate
1 tablespoon shortening
4 ounces semisweet chocolate

Preheat oven to 350° F.

Beat almond paste with sugar until paste is broken up. Add eggs, one at a time and beat at medium speed until light and fluffy. Near the end of mixing, add zest. Mix in flour at low speed until just combined.

Pour batter into a greased and floured cake pan and bake for 18-20 minutes. Remove from oven and cool completely. Remove cake from cake pan and cut into individual shapes with a cookie cutter shaped like a moon.

Meanwhile, place butter, white chocolate, and shortening in a double boiler and heat until fully combined.

Place cakes on a drying rack and coat with white chocolate mixture. Melt semisweet chocolate and drizzle with quick side to side movements over the individual cakes. Allow chocolate to set before serving.

White Chocolate Dotted Swiss Cake

2¼ cups sifted cake flour
1¾ cups sugar
1 tablespoon baking powder
pinch salt

½ cup vegetable oil
5 large egg yolks
1 tablespoon grated orange zest
1 tablespoon vanilla
¾ cup water
5 egg whites
½ teaspoon cream of tartar
1 cup sugar
1 cup water
¼ cup amaretto
½ pint heavy whipping cream
3 cups white chocolate, small chunks
1 jar raspberry jam

Preheat oven to 325° F. Sift flour, sugar, baking powder and salt into mixing bowl. Make a well in center of dry ingredients. Add oil, egg yolks, orange zest and vanilla. Add water, ¼ cup at a time. Beat by hand until batter is smooth and free of lumps.

Beat egg whites and cream of tartar in separate bowl until very stiff. Gently fold into batter. Do not stir. Line three 6" x 2" baking pans with parchment paper. Fill each baking pan ¾ full. Bake for 50 minutes or until toothpick stuck in center comes out clean. Cool. Using metal spatula, go around rim of cake and loosen cake. Turn out and refrigerate at least 2 hours.

Make ganache by heating whipping cream just to the boiling point. Add chopped chocolate and whip until well smooth. Refrigerate until mixture holds its shape and spreads easily. Make simple syrup with 1 cup of sugar and 1 cup of water. Bring to a boil for 5 minutes. Add amaretto.

Assemble cake by horizontally cutting only two layers in half. (Reserve third layer for another use.) Drizzle simple syrup generously over layers, do not soak. Spread first layer with a little raspberry jam and repeat until all layers are stacked and have jam between layers. Frost cake with chocolate ganache. Use remaining ganache in pastry bag with a #4 tip and make dots over all edges of cake. Decorate with flowers as desired.

McCharles House, Tustin, California

THE GREAT TEA ROOMS OF AMERICA

Alice's Tea Cup
102 W. 73rd Street at Columbus Avenue
New York, New York 10023
212.799.3006
www.alicesteacup.com

Butchart Gardens
Box 4010
Victoria, British Columbia V8X 3X4
250.652.8222
www.butchartgardens.com

Cliffside Inn
2 Seaview Avenue
Newport, Rhode Island 02840
401.847.1811
www.cliffsideinn.com

Disney's Grand Floridian Resort & Spa
Walt Disney World Resort
4401 Floridian Way
Lake Buena Vista, Florida 32830
407.939.3463
www.disneyworld.com

The Drake Hotel
140 East Walton Place
Chicago, Illinois 60611
800.553.7253
www.thedrakehotel.com

Dunbar Tea Room
1 Water Street
Sandwich, Massachusetts 02563
Phone 508.833.2485
www.dunbarteashop.com

Dushanbe Teahouse
1770 13th Street
Boulder, Colorado 80302
303.442.4993
www.boulderteahouse.com

The Fairmont Chateau Lake Louise
111 Lake Louise Drive
Lake Louise, Alberta T0L1E0
403.522.3511
www.fairmont.com/lakelouise

The Fairmont Empress Hotel
721 Government Street
Victoria, British Columbia V8W 1 W5
250.384.8111
www.fairmont.com/empress

Grand American Hotel
555 South Main Street
Salt Lake City, UT 84111
801.258.6000
www.grandamerica.com

Lady Mendl's
The Inn at Irving Place
56 Irving Place
New York, New York 10003
212.533.4600
www.innatirving.com

Miss Mable's
301 West College Street
Dickson, Tennessee 37055
615.441.6658
www.missmable.com

Queen Mary Tea Room
2912 NE 55th Street
Seattle, Washington 98105
206.527.2770
www.queenmarytea.com

The Tea Room
7 East Broughton Street
Savannah, Georgia 31401
912.239.9690
www.thetearoomsavannah.com

Rose Tree Cottage
828 E. California Boulevard
Pasadena, California 91106
626.793.3337
www.rosetreecottage.com

Samovar Tea Lounge
489 Sanchez St at 18th Street
San Francisco, California 94114
415.626.4700
www.samovartealounge.com

St. James Tearoom
901 Rio Grande NE Suite E-130
Albuquerque, New Mexico 87104
505.242.3752
www.stjamestearoom.com

St. Regis Hotel
2 East 55th Street
New York, New York 10022
212.753.4500
www.stregis.com

Tea Leaves & Thyme
8990 S. Main Street
Woodstock, Georgia 30188
770-516-2609
www.tealeavesandthyme.com

The Tea Room
7 East Broughton Street
Savannah, Georgia 31401
912.239.9690
www.savannahtearoom.com

Windsor Court Hotel
300 Gravier Street
New Orleans, Louisiana 70130
888.596.0955
www.windsorcourthotel.com

RECIPE INDEX